DEAF DAY by Leslie Ayvazian
"A gentle, enchanting one-woman show."
—ANITA GATES, *The New York Times*

UP, DOWN, STRANGE, CHARMED, BEAUTY, AND TRUTH by Edward Allan Baker
"A wrenching tale of loves found and lost, of broken hearts and betrayal." —LAWRENCE VAN GELDER, *The New York Times*

WAR by Bill Bozzone
"Packs its own goodly share of potent emotion."
—LAWRENCE VAN GELDER, *The New York Times*

THE ONCE ATTRACTIVE WOMAN by Christine Farrell
"A hell of a one-act . . . great fun and well-crafted."
—NICK BRANDI, *Showbusiness*

THE GOLF BALL by Frank D. Gilroy
"A terse, smart, sardonic little script."
—MICHAEL FEINGOLD, *The Village Voice*

GOODBYE, OSCAR by Romulus Linney
"Presents Wilde anew, with charm and poignancy . . . Touching, dignified, and gently witty."
—ROBERT SIMONSON, *Time Out, New York*

MAIDEN LANE by Cassandra Medley
"Most provocative . . . A multilayered look at race and real estate."
—AILEEN JACOBSON, *Newsday*

IN THE WESTERN GARDEN by Stuart Spencer

"The evening's gem . . . Packed into the play's short space are a neat, effective intrigue, a fierce debate about the nature of creativity, [and] four vivid characters."

—MICHAEL FEINGOLD, *The Village Voice*

ALL ABOUT AL by Cherie Vogelstein

"Cheerfully clever." —ANITA GATES, *The New York Times*

THE "I" WORD: INTERNS by Michael Louis Wells

"Wells handles today's Beltway jargon with brains and even a bit of Shavian brio." —MICHAEL FEINGOLD, *The Village Voice*

Ensemble Studio Theatre Marathon '99

› with a foreword by **Curt Dempster**

THE ONE-ACT PLAYS

ff **FABER AND FABER, INC.**
an affiliate of **Farrar, Straus and Giroux**

FABER AND FABER, INC.
An affiliate of Farrar, Straus and Giroux
19 Union Square West, New York 10003

Printed in the United States of America

Library of Congress catalog card number: 1529-5842

Designed by Gretchen Achilles

FIRST EDITION, 2000

Pages 251–52 constitute an extension of this copyright page.

Foreword

In order to grow and develop, playwrights need to have their short plays produced. The work of all major American playwrights can be traced back to their early one-act productions—Eugene O'Neill, Arthur Miller, Tennessee Williams, Edward Albee, John Guare, David Mamet, Sam Shepard, Richard Greenberg, and August Wilson, to name a few.

However, after a brief golden moment in the early days of the Off Broadway movement, the one-act was either consigned to minor status or dismissed as too expensive to produce. In 1977, The Ensemble Studio Theatre set out to rescue the short play from artistic neglect. Each year we choose ten to twelve plays from over a thousand unproduced submissions and premiere them on our mainstage with E.S.T. members and guest artists. We are proud that our annual marathon of one-act plays has gained national and international attention and has brought the short form back to where it belongs—center stage.

This fine new edition of the plays from our 1999 One-Act Marathon marks a new era for our one-acts—an expanded forum so these important plays can find an even wider audience. Whether you, the adventurous reader, are at the professional, amateur, or academic level, we urge you to join the one-act movement by producing some of these short plays or discovering new ones and producing them. By doing so, you will be helping to replenish the theatrical habitat of the American playwright.

—CURT DEMPSTER
New York City, 1999

Contents

Ensemble Studio Theatre Marathon '99

Deaf Day

›LESLIE AYVAZIAN

'99

ORIGINAL PRODUCTION

DIRECTOR Leslie Ayvazian

ASSISTANT DIRECTOR Nina Steiger

SET DESIGNER Kris Stone

COSTUME DESIGNER Amela Baksic

SOUND Beatrice Terry

PROPS Erika Malone

PRODUCTION STAGE MANAGER Gretchen A. Knowlton

STAGE MANAGER Karyn Meek

The cast was as follows:

MOTHER Kaitlyn Kenney

CHARACTERS

DEAF MOTHER, with deaf son, seven years old
Spoken simultaneously in English and sign language

Okay,
Ready?
Come on!
Sun's up, day's here.
Let's go!
Rise and shine.
That means: get up and . . . be happy!
Come on.
Don't ignore me.

Look at me! Yes!

We have to practice English.
Yes. Today is a practice day.
Your teacher said.
So look at me. Look at me!

Put your hearing aids in. Yes!
(Looks at him.)
Now!

Good.

Okay.
We're going to the playground.

No, not at deaf school.
In the park.

Yes, there will be hearing children there.
I don't know if there will be any deaf kids.
You can speak to the hearing children.
Yes, you can.
Sure, you can.

Remember the new boy on our street? Roger!
Maybe we'll see the new boy Roger and his dog!
You can talk to them. Yes!
And to other kids, too.

Yes, you can.

You stand in front of them.
Look directly in their faces.
If they look away, say *(No sign)*, "Could you please repeat that?"
(No sign) "Could you please repeat that?"
(With sign) Yes, you can.
Say *(No sign)*, "I can't hear you because I'm deaf."

(With sign) Some will laugh.
Some won't laugh.
Talk to the ones who don't laugh.
Come on, honey.
Yes.
Put your shoes on.
Put your shoes on!
I'll put them on you!

Then sit down and put them on!

Sit down!

Now tie your shoes.

Good.

Okay.

Get up.

Get up!

Get up!

Look at me!

Don't turn your head away.

Come on.

Okay.

I'll wait.

(She waits. She taps her foot. She looks at him.)

Hi.

Yes, I'll stay in the park with you, of course.

I'll sit on the closest bench.

You can talk to me whenever you want.

People may watch you.

And some may think, *Wow!* Look at this kid!

He knows two languages! How cool!

Well, some will think, *Wow!*

Some might be stupid.

We will ignore the stupid ones.

Do we feel sorry for the stupid ones?

Nah.

We think they're stupid.

But some people will see how wonderful you are.

And those people will want to talk to you.

So watch their faces.

Read their lips.

If they walk away without telling you where they are going, don't
  be mad.

Hearing people talk with their backs to each other.

At those times, wave to me.

We will talk.

And then we'll come home. Yes.

And you can be quiet for as long as you want to be quiet.

No voices. Quiet.

Quiet.

Okay.

You ready?

Hearing aids turned on!

Eyes open!

Let's go!

No, we don't have to march.

We can walk slowly!

We can walk real slowly.

And we'll look at each other.

And we'll talk.

In sign.

We'll talk.

I promise.

(Without sign)

Good.

(Lights shift.)

(Lights come up. It's the same day: evening.)

Hey.

It's almost time for bed!

Yes, it is!

And you have sleepy eyes.

Yes, yes, yes, you do.

But first . . .

Look at me, honey.

(Hits floor for his attention.)

(In sign) Look at me! Good.

(In sign and English) Let's practice English before we go to bed.

Practice Day is nearly finished.

Watch my face.

Come on, watch.

Let's talk about the park.

No. No Roger! No dog. No.

But the seesaw! Yes!

That girl!

No, we don't know her name.

But you two were perfectly balanced!

You sat in the air at the same time!

That's very special.

But the slide. I know.

They pushed you down the slide.

They wanted you to go faster.
They said, *Hey! Hey!*

They didn't know that you couldn't hear them.
So they pushed.
They pushed hard. I know.

It surprised you.
And it hurt you. I know.

They pushed you because they were frustrated with you.

But I think you can understand.
Sure you can.
Think about your deaf friends at school.
When you want their attention, sometimes you grab them. Sometimes you hit them. Sure you do.
Because you want them to look at you.
And you get frustrated. Yes, you do!

So next time, if the kids are waiting, you go fast!
Okay!
Go fast down that slide.
You kick butt!
Yes!

Then no one will push you.
And no one will laugh.
You need to be fast and quick, quick, quick.
Like a bunny.
Yes.

A fast bunny who kicks butt!
That's you!

Yes!
Right! Jackie Chan!

Okay.
(*Jumps up and does Jackie Chan stance.*)
Jackie Chan!

Auhhhhhh!
(*Does tae kwon do kick.*)
We are Jackie Chan!
(*Another move.*)
But you have sleepy eyes!

Yes.

Cherry ut. Cun yay. (*Bows to him.*) Tae kwon.

So get in bed, Jackie Chan.

And maybe tomorrow we'll go to the planetarium.

Or the zoo?

Maybe the park. And you can get back in the saddle.

That means: When you ride a horse and fall off, you need to get
back on the horse right away. So you don't feel scared.

Back in the saddle.
Back in the park.
Back on the slide.
Okay?

Okay.

Now sleep, honey.
Sweet dreams.
(She waves.)
Sweet dreams.
(She leaves his room and sits. She waits. Then she gets back up and goes to his room. She sees he is still awake but sleepy. She waves again. She leaves and goes back to her chair. She waits. Then she goes again and checks on him. He's asleep. She returns to her chair and sits. She breathes a sigh of relief. Beat. She notices he has walked into the room.)
What's up?

Tomorrow?

Stay home?

All day?

No voices?

Quiet?

I'm thinking.
(She gets up and sits on the floor.)

Okay.

Tomorrow.

Quiet.

I promise.

Yes.

(In sign) Quiet. Quiet. I promise.
(In sign and English) Good night.
(In just sign) Good night.
(She sits watching her son.)

(Lights fade.)

Up, Down, Strange, Charmed, Beauty, and Truth

'99

> EDWARD ALLAN BAKER

ORIGINAL PRODUCTION

DIRECTOR Ron Stetson

ASSISTANT DIRECTOR Nancy Wu

SET DESIGNER Carlo Adinolfi

COSTUME DESIGNER Austin Sanderson

SOUND Robert Gould

PROPS Erika Malone

MAKEUP Jay Pearlman

PRODUCTION STAGE MANAGER Gail Eve Malatesta

STAGE MANAGER Leisah Swenson

The cast was as follows:

MARLEY Amy Love

DANNY Bruce MacVittie

STEPH Amy Staats

This play is for Marlena Olga Rose

CHARACTERS

DANNY

MARLEY

STEPH

PLACE

East Providence, Rhode Island

TIME

Autumn 1998

SETTING

A small dining room not overly furnished and dominated by a dining-room table with mismatched chairs. There is a stereo in a cluttered bookshelf, a phone on an end table, a small sofa, a soft-cushioned chair. A door to a bedroom is in the upper-left corner, an opening to the kitchen and to the outside is stage left.

PRE-SHOW AND POST-SHOW MUSIC

Should consist of soulful selections from female solo artists of 1998–99.

"For every atom belonging to me as good belongs to you."

—WALT WHITMAN

Lights up on DANNY *(forty) and* MARLEY *(sixteen) at the den table, schoolbooks and notebooks in front of them.* DANNY *is wearing a baseball cap, T-shirt, paint-splattered jeans, and cheap canvas shoes with no socks.* MARLEY *is dressed modestly. No fashion statement from her. It's mid-afternoon.*

MARLEY C'mon, Uncle Danny . . . find it.

(DANNY *is flipping through a textbook.*)

DANNY I'm lookin'. I'm lookin' . . .

MARLEY The heading is "Chaos."

DANNY You told me that.

MARLEY C-H-A-O-S.

DANNY I know how to spell it. I got to the ninth grade, in case you didn't know it.

MARLEY You only got to the ninth grade?

DANNY Well, yunno, I *was* twenty-five years old.

MARLEY And in the ninth grade?!

DANNY I could beat the shit out of everybody.

MARLEY Please tell me you're kidding . . .

DANNY I can't, honey, 'cause then my nieces and nephews wouldn't enjoy me as much if they knew the truth of my— Found it— Chaos—

MARLEY Ask me anything.

DANNY All right . . . um . . . Let's see, you already know how to spell it, um, okay . . . uh . . . "A chaotic system is one in which the final outcome depends on—" what?

MARLEY Oh . . . uh . . . I—I know this . . . uh, God . . . uh . . .

DANNY . . . the final outcome depends on what?

MARLEY I . . . I . . . I can't think . . . I know the answer, but there's like, *like a wall in front of it!*

DANNY Hey hey hey, calm down, what'sa matter? It's only a test, c'mon relax. Have a sip a beer, a smoke . . .

MARLEY I'm all right . . .

DANNY You want a beer? Shot a vodka? Some crack?

MARLEY What?!

DANNY Just trying to get back the smile—

MARLEY I don't feel like smiling.

DANNY *(Closes the book.)* No smile, no help from Uncle Danny.

MARLEY All right, I'll smile. I—I have to ace this test. *(She smiles.)* Okay, give me the answer— *No no wait*—"A chaotic system is one—in which—in which the final outcome depends on—depends on—*on the initial conditions!*" *(DANNY jumps up to do an "end zone" dance. He downs his beer. Crushes the can. Tosses it.)* Okay, okay now . . . I wrote out an example. *(Hands him notebook.)* Follow along with me—*(Beat.)* "White water in a stream is a good example of a chaotic system . . ."

(Beat—beat.)

DANNY There's more.

MARLEY *(Snaps at him.)* I know that!

DANNY Wow, this is a lot of fun.

MARLEY Sorry, sorry.

DANNY You're worse than your mother flyin' off the handle like that.

MARLEY *(Pointedly)* I'm *not* my mother.

DANNY No. Now you're *my* mother.

MARLEY Let's keep going.

DANNY But you got me afraid.

MARLEY ". . . if you put . . . if you start a chip of wood at one position, it will come out at a certain point" . . . um . . . "on the other side of a rapids . . ."

DANNY Good good . . .

MARLEY "If you start the second chip of wood at a position not quite the same to the first, the second chip—the second chip" . . . um . . .

DANNY *(Interrupts her.)* Don't you want to keep saying "chip of wood" instead of just "chip"? 'Cause "chip" is like—are you now talking about a potato chip, you know what I'm saying?

(MARLEY stares at him for a moment.)

MARLEY How could I go from talking about "chips of wood" as an example to potato chips?!

DANNY If I'm the one listening, say, I might get confused. *(MARLEY looks at him in disbelief.)* All right, forget it, forget it . . .

MARLEY God . . .

DANNY Okay, you left off with um . . . um . . . All right, start right after "If you start the second chip of wood—"

MARLEY "—at a position not quite the same as the first, the *second chip of wood* will come out of the rapids *far* from where the first one did." Is that right?

DANNY Yeah sure, but what's the big deal here? I don't get it.

MARLEY I said everything right?

DANNY Yeah. You just gave the example of—of—

MARLEY Of the chaotic system and how the final outcome depends on the initial conditions, *Yes!*

DANNY Why's this test so important?

MARLEY If I ace this test, I go to High Honors, which gets me all kinds of scholarships for colleges far away from here. Get out of this—this crazy house. Can't breathe here. So hard to breathe at night—here.

DANNY What the hell you going on about?

MARLEY If I don't ace this test—

DANNY It's not the end of the world.

(Pause.)

MARLEY How old were you when you first had sex?

DANNY *(After a beat.)* I haven't had sex yet.

MARLEY No, really.

DANNY How did we get on this all of a sudden?

MARLEY How old were you?

DANNY Let's see, ninth grade, probly. In fact, I'm sure, 'cause it was
with my homeroom teacher.

MARLEY How come you never give straight answers?

DANNY And she was a nun.

MARLEY You had sex with a . . . ?!

DANNY *(Stands.)* Just pull the wimple down over the face—

MARLEY Gross! Stop, stop!

DANNY For five minutes I was Jesus and she was Carmella
Peckarinni—

MARLEY *(Laughs out loud.)* All right, enough, enough!

STEPH *(Yells from another room)* Marley! Be quiet! God!

DANNY *(After a beat.)* What is she doing home? *(MARLEY shrugs.)*
Steph? Why aren't you at work?

STEPH *(From other room)* Got a headache.

DANNY *(To MARLEY)* That true?

MARLEY *(Vaguely)* Guess.

DANNY Go get me another beer. We'll keep going with this stuff.
*(MARLEY goes to the kitchen. DANNY goes to STEPH's bedroom door.
Knocks softly.)* Steph?

STEPH *(From behind the door)* Leave me alone, Uncle Danny. Go help
Marley get smarter. I'm just the piece-a-shit daughter.

DANNY Not to me. To me you're my . . . piece-a-shit niece. *(Silence.)* Steph, I'm kidding. (MARLEY *re-enters with a can of beer. She
hands it to* DANNY. *She returns to the table.* DANNY *opens the beer.)*
What's going on with her?

MARLEY I really think she has to be the one to—

DANNY Give me the short version 'fore I smack ya.

MARLEY She and my mother had a fight.

DANNY Okay.

MARLEY A real bad one.

DANNY I remember those.

MARLEY Ma caught Steph having sex last night. Walked in on her.

DANNY Where?

MARLEY Here.

DANNY Here?

MARLEY In our room.

DANNY Jesus . . .

MARLEY You know what the funny thing was?

DANNY There's a *funny* in this?

MARLEY Ma came home with a guy.

DANNY Guy she's been going with—Ray?

MARLEY Newer guy.

DANNY Why's that funny?

MARLEY Because, duh, she came back here to have sex with him.

DANNY You don't know that.

MARLEY Uncle Danny, this is your sister we're talking about. Don't act dumb on this one.

DANNY What the hell does that mean?

MARLEY It means my mother doesn't bring guys home just to wallpaper the living room.

DANNY All right, all right, don't get smart here, she's still your mother . . .

MARLEY It's why sometimes I think me and Steph have different fathers—

DANNY (*After a beat.*) Okay, let's drop this and get back to the— uh—the—uh—chaos stuff for the test—

MARLEY *(Hands him a paper.)* Okay, ask me the definitions from this sheet.

DANNY Okay, what is G.U.T.?

MARLEY Grand Unified Theory.

DANNY T.O.E.?

MARLEY Theory of Everything.

DANNY And this little theory of everything went to market, and this little theory of everything stayed home—

MARLEY What's the next one?

DANNY Just so happens it's one of my favorite words—quark.

MARLEY Quarks are locked into particles . . . um . . . you can't see them and . . . uh . . .

DANNY "Elementary particles" is written here.

MARLEY Okay, okay . . .

DANNY How many quarks are there?

MARLEY Six. "Up, Down, Strange, Charmed, Bottom, and Top," unless—and this is for bonus points—unless you come from Harvard, in which case it's "Up, Down, Strange, Charmed, Beauty, and Truth."

DANNY I like the Harvard way, don't you?

MARLEY Who cares. Keep going.

DANNY There are three kinds of leptons called—

MARLEY Neutrinos and and these . . . um . . . particles have no mass, no electrical charge, and travel at the speed of light.

DANNY Shit, if they don't weigh anythin' and don't do anythin' and move that f'n fast, how do you know they're there?

MARLEY Where's that question?

DANNY I'm asking it.

MARLEY Oh, that's something you learn in the tenth grade. Sorry, Uncle Danny.

DANNY I can take it.

MARLEY Next question.

DANNY Were you here when Steph brought home the guy to do the "nasty"?

MARLEY Um . . .

DANNY Yes? No? Probly why your mother flipped out on her, 'cause you were in the house.

MARLEY I don't think so.

DANNY Were you here when Steph was?

MARLEY Yup.

DANNY Did you know what was going on?

MARLEY I'm sixteen.

DANNY Yeah, and five minutes ago you asked me when I had sex for the first time like you was twelve. I mean, is that something a sixteen-year-old asks her favorite uncle?

MARLEY You think you're my favorite uncle?

DANNY All right, all right, let's stop here—

MARLEY I'm kidding, I'm kidding!

DANNY Did you know what was going on with Steph and—

MARLEY No, not really.

DANNY So you was surprised the same time your mother was?

MARLEY Yup.

DANNY Just trying to get a bead on this whole thing that happened with—

MARLEY *(Cuts him off.)* Let's just keep doing the—

DANNY Forget it for now. You got a whole night to study.

MARLEY God, she got caught, they had a fight, and . . . *Steph! Steph!*

(Pause. STEPH, *nineteen, enters the den from her bedroom. Her pretty face is quite bruised, scratches visible around her neck and arms, and she looks as if she slept in her jeans and T-shirt all night.* DANNY *looks at her, motionless. After a silence.)*

STEPH Marley didn't need you to study with her. I made her call you. We both knew you'd come for her.

DANNY I would've come for you. You didn't have to make something up to get me here.

STEPH It's what I do best. Make things up.

DANNY How come you didn't come out when I got here?

STEPH *(Shrugs.)* Tired. Ashamed. Then got chicken to talk with you. When you were at the door, I was crying inside, you know, 'cause I wanted, so much for you to break the door down and—

DANNY Steph . . .

STEPH Don't come near me. I smell.

DANNY So do I.

STEPH No, really, don't come close.

DANNY Can I clean up your face?

STEPH I don't want it clean.

DANNY Could get infected.

STEPH Good.

DANNY Don't say that!

MARLEY Steph, you want some coffee?

STEPH Yeah.

MARLEY Heat it up in the microwave okay or should I make some fresh?

STEPH Zappin' it is okay.

(MARLEY goes to the kitchen. DANNY goes to the table. Picks up his cigarettes.)

DANNY You want a smoke?

(STEPH keeps her distance from DANNY.)

STEPH No, I quit two weeks ago—uh—two weeks this Thursday, great, huh? Me and a friend at work made a deal to do it.

(DANNY puts his cigarette back in the pack.)

DANNY Good. That's good, Steph.

STEPH Yeah, I'm proud of it.

DANNY I figured if I quit I'd just be getting secondhand smoke, so why not keep smoking and get the best.

(STEPH *doesn't move from the corner she's in.*)

STEPH No one would ever know you're a part of this crazy family, which includes my mother.

DANNY Well, I am. And so are you.

STEPH She told me to move out today. *(Beat.)* But I . . . I can't leave Marley and . . . She and me been puttin' up with Ma all these—these years and—and Marley doesn't know about her father not being—

DANNY Not being "Birdman."

STEPH We been going on like "Birdman" is both our fathers and . . .

DANNY *(Cuts her off.)* I know all about it.

STEPH And I called him late last night—but he wants nothing to do with us, you know. He got sobered up, has a new family . . .

(MARLEY *re-enters the den. Hands* STEPH *a cup of coffee.*)

STEPH Thanks. Put on some of your pretty music.

(MARLEY *goes to the stereo.* DANNY *goes to* STEPH.)

DANNY Well, whadda we do? What happens next? You want me to talk to your mother? What? You won't let me fix up your face or hold you, so we just . . . what?

(*Classical music comes up softly.*)

STEPH I—I figured some stuff out . . . or yunno . . . have this plan of you helpin' us . . . me and Marley.

DANNY Yeah, how?

STEPH First of all, did Marley tell you everything that happened last night?

MARLEY I didn't tell him the part about—

DANNY *(Cuts her off.)* She told me your mother caught you having sex.

MARLEY That's all I got to.

STEPH It was more than that.

DANNY You don't hafta tell me if you don't want, all right? It's kinda none of my business, okay? I believe in that, all right, but if my daughter was still around and I came home and caught her doing what you—

STEPH *(Cuts him off.)* It was with a girl. *(Beat.)* She's um . . . my girlfriend. Named Dawn. One I work with. One who quit smoking with me.

(Silence for a few beats.)

DANNY Oh.

STEPH We got close, yunno, and—uh—talk and laugh like crazy and dance. I mean, she has a tough life . . . um . . . a tough life, too, and I don't know, guys just . . . guys just freak me out, okay? They just do. Stupid games and shit, and just want . . . um . . . just want one thing and—

DANNY *(Cuts her off.)* Okay, hold it, hold it. Let's just stop here for a minute. I gotta take this in for a minute, okay? Gimme a minute.

MARLEY Uncle Danny, you need a minute?

DANNY I'm serious here.

STEPH You think I'm sick 'cause I slept with a girl?

DANNY No.

MARLEY You shouldn't have told him.

STEPH It makes me a bad person, yunno, sick?

(DANNY looks at MARLEY.)

DANNY What do you think of this . . . of what she just said?

MARLEY I don't think she's sick.

DANNY *(After a beat.)* That's it?!

MARLEY She's my sister.

(DANNY turns to STEPH.)

DANNY *Now* I understand your mother bein' upset like she was, I mean, bein' with a guy is one thing, but the shock of seeing you with a girl, I mean, what the hell were you thinkin' even carrying on in here?!

STEPH Me and Marley were here alone and I ran out to get us a video and I bumped into Dawn and then we—yunno—came back here and—

DANNY *(Turns away.)* Okay, okay . . .

STEPH I love her, Uncle Danny . . .

DANNY Yup, yup . . .

STEPH And to be with the one you love in your own bedroom where for so many nights I only imagined being with her . . . I—I couldn't help it. We had candles and incense burning and I—I lost all sense of where I was, you know? I forgot about everything . . . but her and . . .

DANNY I don't need to hear this, Steph . . .

(STEPH bangs the table with both hands.)

STEPH Well, I need to say it, 'cause the flip side was so— *(Breaks down some.)*

(MARLEY runs to turn off the music. Goes to STEPH.)

MARLEY It was bad, Uncle Danny.

STEPH The door burst open. The light came on. I could see Ma's eyes after a second turn to fire, which was probly the candle reflection, but—um—she and this soft-looking fat fuck of a guy next to her was grinning, and I . . . sat up fast and she punched me so hard in the face that I went down as Dawn was coming up, and we smashed our heads together, and all I could taste was blood. Then I . . . I felt my hair being yanked and what she did was, she lifted me outta the bed by my hair, and feeling like a fucking rag doll, I was all of a sudden up against my wall and—and her hands were around my throat and I thought she was going to kill me and I—I could hear Dawn—uh—screaming, and outta one eye I saw Marley at the door, and honest to God, I—I wanted to die, and that soft-looking fat fuck of a guy was— *(Beat.)* He was . . .

MARLEY Hitting on Dawn.

STEPH Slappin' her hard.

MARLEY And she got sick all over the bed.

STEPH And Marley turned off the light—

MARLEY I couldn't think of anything else to do!

STEPH Then it was like bein' in the—yunno—at the amusement park in the House of Horror, and you hear screams way off in the distance? When the light came back on I saw Dawn being shoved outta the room by that soft-looking fat fuck of a guy. Then Ma opened my closet and threw me in—put a chair against the door . . .

DANNY *(Softly)* I remember my mother doin' that to her.

STEPH What?

MARLEY He said he remembers Nana doing that to Ma.

DANNY *(Softly)* Unbelievable. *(Pause.)* I'll talk with her.

STEPH I don't want you to.

DANNY What?

STEPH No more talking to her.

DANNY Whaddaya mean?

STEPH I mean . . . *(Takes a breath.)* I mean she's a fucking loser, okay, a person who cares only about herself gettin' off, all right, somebody who never should've had kids, a—a person who one night last week had me and Marley scrub the walls and floors while she was at that table scraping the black shit, the resin stuff, outta her dope pipe that she smoked . . .

MARLEY It smelled so bad.

STEPH She'll do anything to get off, anything to get money.

MARLEY That time we were living in Aunt Alice's basement, remember?

STEPH She went into her own sister's bedroom and stole money while Aunt Alice was at work, and told us she'd put it back when she got it. Even took a ring. "Oh, this is mine."

MARLEY That was a lie.

STEPH Uncle Danny, she's forty-six and real desperate, and shit, you know? She's gotten fat, won't work a real job, and the type a guy she brings home now is . . . like her. And what scares me is me not being here and something happening to Marley, you know what I'm saying? *(Beat—beat.)* She screamed I had to move out tomorrow, which is today . . . but I can't leave Marley here alone . . . I won't do that. *(She stands behind* MARLEY.*)* Uncle Danny, okay, this girl has a future and I'm afraid it'll be ruined if . . . if something bad happens. So what do I do? *(Beat.)* We're afraid.

*(*DANNY *stares at the two girls. Silence.)*

DANNY *(Finally)* Sit down for a minute while I clean your face up. Marley, wet me a facecloth. Get some disinfectant. *(The girls remain still. He claps his hands to get them moving.* MARLEY *goes to the kitchen after getting the okay from* STEPH.*)* C'mon, get over here, sit. *(*STEPH *moves to the table and sits. Arms crossed. He stands behind her. Stays fixed on her.)* There was this guy who had this bird who made too much noise, so one day he takes it outta its cage and throws it in the freezer. The bird starts cryin', "Please, please let me out, I'll be quiet." So the guy takes it out. The bird looks at him and says, "Not for nothin', but what did the chicken do?" *(He leans down to an upset-looking* STEPH.*)* "Not for nothin', but what did the chicken do?"

*(*STEPH *loses it. Turns and wraps her arms around* DANNY's *waist and hugs him. He strokes her back, caringly.)*

STEPH (*After a beat.*) I'm sorry.

DANNY For what?

STEPH For throwin' this shit at you.

DANNY I'm a good target for shit.

STEPH You got your own troubles.

DANNY Things are picking up. (*Beat.*) I got cable now.

STEPH Never understood why Aunt Lynn up and left you like she did.

(DANNY *releases her. Gets some distance.*)

DANNY Don't go makin' me out to be some kinda saint, okay?

STEPH And I'm sorry she took Danielle with her.

DANNY Won't be forever.

(MARLEY *returns with facecloth and disinfectant. Gives them to* DANNY.)

MARLEY Steph, should I pack my stuff?

DANNY Why, where you going? (*He starts to clean* STEPH's *face with facecloth.*)

MARLEY Away from here.

DANNY Relax. You're not going anywhere.

(MARLEY *and* STEPH *exchange eye contact.*)

STEPH (*To* MARLEY) Sit for now.

DANNY I'm going to straighten this all out with your mother.

STEPH You think so?

DANNY I know so.

STEPH And she'll drop to her knees begging for forgiveness, learn how to cook, learn how to work for a living, learn how to talk to her daughters, go to a rehab, stop stealin' and stop lyin', then stop pickin' up guys who are losers she finds in bars for losers?

(DANNY *continues working on her face.*)

DANNY Stop talking for a minute.

STEPH (*After a beat.*) You miss Danielle?

MARLEY She was my favorite cousin.

DANNY I don't wanna talk about it.

STEPH How come?

MARLEY Steph . . .

STEPH Just blocking it out?

DANNY Yeah.

STEPH That's not good, right?

MARLEY Steph . . .

STEPH You ever wonder where they are?

(DANNY *backs away from* STEPH. *Annoyed*)

DANNY Whadda ya trying to pull here?

STEPH Nothing.

DANNY You had a bad night, don't go pullin' my troubles into the mix.

STEPH One morning you wake up—and they're gone. No note. No nothing.

DANNY That's enough, Steph.

STEPH Why? You, the nicest man, loses his family while my mother gets to—

(DANNY *pounds on the table with his fists, scaring* MARLEY *and* STEPH.)

DANNY *I said that's enough! Okay?! I've had it! No more talking on what happened three years ago!*

(*Brief silence.*)

MARLEY I've never seen you get mad before.

DANNY Uncle Danny isn't what he seems to you kids . . .

STEPH Did you hit Aunt Lynn?

DANNY Why are you pushin' this?

STEPH I just want to know.

DANNY Well, I don't want you to—

STEPH Is that why she left?

DANNY It makes no difference! She left!

MARLEY Steph, c'mon . . .

STEPH Did you hit her?!

DANNY *(Suddenly)* Once! Open hand! Hard as I could! *(Beat.)* Over something stupid.

STEPH If she came back tomorrow, would you change?

DANNY Let's stop this right now, okay? No more talkin' about me, okay. That's enough of that shit! I'm doin' just fine . . . Paintin' cars for a livin' and playin' softball on weekends! *(He drinks some beer. Girls watch him.)* Life goes on, just like it will here, and we'll eat, shit, and watch TV—*(He starts for the phone.)* Now, your mother's at work, right?

STEPH You're not goin' to call her.

DANNY Oh no?

STEPH No.

(DANNY picks up the phone.)

DANNY Uncle Danny's goin' to fix this, 'cause I love you two and I'll make sure—

STEPH *No more talking to her!*

(DANNY stops to look at STEPH. After a beat, he hangs up the phone.)

DANNY I hafta ask this, it just came into my head . . . Did you kill her?

MARLEY *(Laughs.)* God . . .

STEPH Nope.

DANNY You turn her in to the cops?

STEPH Nope.

MARLEY *(Laughs more.)* Imagine doing that to Ma.

DANNY Then whaddaya talkin' about, Steph?! Stop f'n around with me. You got something to say, then—

STEPH I have a way, a plan for getting all of us to a new place, a new life. Me, Marley, Dawn, and you, Uncle Danny. Another chance.

MARLEY Dawn?

(STEPH gets a bit closer to DANNY.)

STEPH We know where Aunt Lynn and Danielle are.

DANNY *(After a beat.)* What?

STEPH You can be at Danielle's sixteenth birthday party. *(Beat—beat.)* If you agree to help us, we'll give you the letter Danielle wrote me and Marley.

DANNY *(Softly)* Are you shittin' me?

MARLEY You never said Dawn was coming with us. Steph?

(MARLEY moves away from the table. STEPH moves closer to DANNY.)

STEPH I don't think you'd ever hit Aunt Lynn again, do you? I don't think you'd ever let that feeling come back, because you'll always remember what it was like to be without them, don't you think? And don't you want to say that to them, huh?

DANNY When did you get this letter?

MARLEY In the summer.

DANNY And you didn't tell me?!

STEPH A secret kept between cousins.

DANNY I should've been told, goddamn it!

MARLEY I wanted to tell you.

STEPH But I wasn't going to do anything until I found out what made them leave you. Danielle never said in the letter—just that she misses you and prays her mother will change her mind and come back here.

(Pause.)

MARLEY Uncle Danny, you okay?

DANNY *(After a beat.)* Yes, I will have another beer, thank you. *(MARLEY goes to the kitchen. DANNY sits.)* Where are they?

STEPH We gotta agree on some stuff first.

(MARLEY re-enters. Gives DANNY his beer. He opens it immediately. Drinks.)

DANNY What stuff?

STEPH Just that you're going along.

DANNY To steal my sister's kids? To take 'em without hearin' her side of this crazy story?

STEPH You don't think it happened?

DANNY I gotta keep rememberin' you're kids and kids blow things way up, and I need to talk to your mother before any runnin' away happens. Is that gettin' through to you?!

(STEPH *glares at him.*)

STEPH Well, we're outta here anyway—*(Looks at* MARLEY.*)* One suitcase. That's all you can take. (MARLEY *goes to the bedroom.* STEPH *looks at* DANNY.*)* We're goin' anyway . . . don't care if we hafta live in a tree, sleep under porches.

DANNY Okay, okay, let me hear this plan a yours. C'mon, spill it out, let's hear it. Me, a sixteen-year-old, and a lesbian couple are cruisin' down Route 95, and—

STEPH *(Cuts him off.)* Thought you might be happy to have a chance to get outta here and be back with your wife and daughter.

DANNY And you really believe the four of us can just go and—

STEPH *Yes!* (DANNY *paces some.* STEPH *watches him.*) Uncle Danny . . .

DANNY I'm sorry you got beat up, and that goes for your friend, too. That's not right, but—

STEPH There's a door open just a little bit.

DANNY It's my oldest sister's kids!

STEPH You mean to tell me you don't believe what I been telling you about her, and how much worse she's getting?

DANNY Still . . . you're her kids! I know the feeling when you lose a kid all of a sudden!

STEPH No comparison between you and her—

DANNY How did all this happen, huh? It happened 'cause your mother caught you in bed with a girl and she freaked out!

STEPH We've been thinking a leaving before last night. We talk about it every fucking day.

DANNY And your plan is to—

STEPH Go with you to where Aunt Lynn is and settle there. I'm going to hit "Birdman" up for some money, pick up my check at Stop & Shop, pick up Dawn . . . then we go.

DANNY How far?

STEPH A thousand miles away.

DANNY Where are they? Japan?

STEPH A *thousand* miles away.

DANNY Canada?

STEPH Uncle Danny . . .

DANNY What?

STEPH You gotta do this.

DANNY Snap. We go.

STEPH Snap. We go.

(DANNY sits.)

DANNY *(After a beat.)* What if she doesn't take me back?

STEPH Well, you're goin' to have to clean up a little. Put on some socks. Ditch the hat. Get a haircut. Flash that great Uncle Danny smile. Talk to her the way you really feel, and think about being with Danielle on her sixteenth birthday.

DANNY *(Looks up at her.)* Are you lyin' to me? Huh? Is this all a made-up story to get easygoing Uncle Danny to do whatever you ask, huh?

STEPH No, it's all—

DANNY *(Cuts her off.)* I was around your mother when she was your age, and you're more like her than you think!

STEPH Don't say that!

DANNY She had a story for every f'n time she got caught at something, and she didn't care how far out it was, man, she'd just keep to it. Is that what you're pullin' with me right now?!

STEPH *I'm not her!*

DANNY Would do anything to avoid the truth . . .

STEPH That's not what I'm doing!

DANNY Sure feels like it.

(STEPH *moves closer to* DANNY.)

STEPH You're worried Aunt Lynn won't take you back, that's why you're—

DANNY *(Cuts her off.)* Oh, now you're inside a my head, right?

STEPH No, I can see it in your face.

(*They lock eyes for a beat or two.*)

DANNY *(Finally)* Let me see this letter you got.

(*They maintain eye contact.*)

STEPH I-am-not-my-mother.

DANNY Let me see this letter.

(*After another beat* STEPH *goes to the bedroom.* DANNY *sits, waits.* STEPH *re-enters the den. Hands him the letter. He stares at it for a moment. Opens it. Reads a little. Tears well up in his eyes.*)

STEPH *(Softly)* It's real.

DANNY *(Softly)* Yeah, I—I . . . uh . . . it's Winnie-the-Pooh . . . *(Smiles.)*—on the top of the—

STEPH Right. Danielle is a Winnie-the-Pooh fanatic.

DANNY Right, right, that's the word for it.

STEPH She's a thousand miles away.

(DANNY *looks at the front of the letter.*)

DANNY Tampa, Florida . . .

STEPH Route 95 all the way.

DANNY I never been outta this state.

STEPH Snap. We go.

DANNY *(After a beat.)* Snap. We go. *(He stands. Paces some. Looks at* STEPH.*)* I—uh—I'm gonna try this. I'm—I'm gonna go, I mean, you know, what the hell, but . . . no way am I bringing Marley.

STEPH What?

DANNY I'll bring you and your little girlfriend, but I'm not takin' Marley . . .

STEPH The whole reason for doing this is to get Marley out of here and—

DANNY Wrong, okay?!

STEPH How is that wrong?!

DANNY It's to get you outta—

STEPH *And* Marley!

DANNY I'm not takin' her, bottom f'n line, Steph! Soon as your mother finds out Marley is gone, she'll call the cops, and I get busted for takin' a minor over the state line, and then where does that leave us, huh?

STEPH I can't be apart from her!

DANNY Then don't go.

STEPH I have to go!

DANNY I can't take her, do you understand?

STEPH *(After a beat.)* This is fucked, you know that, right? *(Beat.)* The next time will be her hitting on Marley, is that what you want?!

DANNY Has she ever hit on Marley?

STEPH What?

DANNY Don't "what" me—has she ever hit on Marley like she does with you?

STEPH No, but she's . . . she's so far gone that I . . . Uncle Danny, listen. Oh God. *(Cries.)* Don't make me go through what you went through when you lost Danielle.

(DANNY gets close to STEPH.)

DANNY It's not the same, 'cause I was thinkin' it was to be forever, all right, and—and Marley will finish school here and—

STEPH God, God, no—

DANNY *And* maybe go to college down there—

STEPH I never been away from her for more than a day—

DANNY I know, Steph, I know . . .

STEPH We got each other through all this—this shit. All the screams in the night, the living in projects, and once for a week after getting evicted we slept under the bleachers over at Dexter Field, and it's—it's where Marley had her first period, okay, and Ma says, "Take her to the pond and clean her up and tell her what she's in for from here on in." *(Beat.)* What if I hadn't been there for her?

DANNY She's goin' to be fine. Hey, she's the smartest one to ever come outta this family. *(Beat.)* Now . . . I'm going to get my stuff, gas up, won't be long. I'll beep three times—

(MARLEY re-enters the den with a suitcase.)

MARLEY So hard figuring out what to put in one suitcase . . . but mostly summer things.

STEPH *(Softly)* Oh yeah?

DANNY *(To STEPH)* If you don't come out—

STEPH Uncle Danny . . .

DANNY If I see—*(Looks at MARLEY.)* I drive off.

MARLEY What's going on with you two? *(With letter in hand DANNY exits. MARLEY follows him for a few steps, then turns to STEPH.)* He's not going to go, is he?

STEPH Um . . .

MARLEY You showed him the letter, didn't you?

STEPH Yup.

MARLEY What did he say?

STEPH Huh?

MARLEY He didn't believe it was from Danielle?

STEPH No, he did.

MARLEY Are we going or not?

STEPH *(After a beat.)* He . . . doesn't want to take you.

MARLEY No, he has—has to mean Dawn. He doesn't want to bring Dawn. He's just mixed up, right?

STEPH He never mentioned anything about not bringing Dawn.

MARLEY So she's going and not me?

STEPH I—I don't know, I'm kind of mixed up right now, okay. Don't talk for a—a minute. *(She picks up the pack of cigarettes* DANNY *left. Removes one. Lights a match. Pauses. Stares at the flame.)*

MARLEY What are we going to do, Steph? You going to answer me?

*(*STEPH *blows out the flame. Puts back the cigarette.)*

STEPH Marley . . .

MARLEY You want to leave without me, don't you?

STEPH No, I don't.

MARLEY But you're going to. I can see it in your eyes. We can tell this kind of stuff with each other, we always could and now—

STEPH He doesn't want to bring you, what can I say, and *I have to get the fuck outta here! (She moves away from* MARLEY, *upset. Yells) Shit! Shit! Shit! Goddamn motherfucker! Shit! Fuck! Shit!*

MARLEY This is all because of Dawn, I'll bet you anything it is!

STEPH Why do you keep saying that? Christ!

MARLEY Everything was fine between me and you till you started going out with her!

STEPH That's bullshit, plus she's not the problem right now, okay! Uncle Danny is. *(She gets closer to* MARLEY.*)* And he . . . he doesn't wanna bring you probly 'cause you're too young and he's still freaked out about his—his daughter leaving him, and Ma's his sister, and he—I don't know—I just know he said no way is he bringing you and—

MARLEY *(Cuts her off.)* Then me and you go alone, the hell with him, right? Right, Steph?

STEPH Listen to me . . .

MARLEY That's what we said we'd do if he didn't want to go.

STEPH Stop for a second and listen to me! *(She takes* MARLEY's *hand.)* I know we talked about leavin', but think about it for a minute. I mean, how far would we get?

MARLEY You're going to back out on me, I can see it, Steph!

STEPH You gotta calm down, you gotta—

*(*MARLEY *moves away from* STEPH.*)*

MARLEY You're going to leave me here! You're going to pick up Dawn, then you're going, aren't you?!

STEPH I don't want to, believe me, I don't . . .

MARLEY *I hate her! I fucking hate her! I wish that fat fuck last night had killed her!*

STEPH Don't say that!

MARLEY She took you away from me, and now she's going to take you far away from me!

STEPH She's not taking me anywhere!

MARLEY Would you go without her?! Huh? *Answer me, lez-bo! Would you leave without her?*

*(*STEPH *freezes. They hold eye contact.* STEPH *brings her hand to her chest—slowly takes a step toward* MARLEY.*)*

STEPH Oh God. You . . . you called Ma last night, didn't you? *(Steps closer to* MARLEY.*)* You told Ma I was here with Dawn.

MARLEY You were forgetting about me!

STEPH How could you do—

MARLEY *(Cuts her off.)* You came in with her, threw me the video, and I could hear you two laughing like we used to laugh, and I could smell the incense *I* got you for your birthday and I—

(STEPH *goes for* MARLEY. *Grabs her by the hair and lifts her from the chair.*)

STEPH *You sonofabitch. They coulda killed us last night! How could you stand at that door and watch what they did? (She gets* MARLEY *to the couch and puts her hands around* MARLEY'S *throat and starts to choke her.) How could you do that to me? To me? (After a few beats she backs away and stares at her trembling hands. Softly)* Jesus Christ . . . (MARLEY *coughs some, then grabs* STEPH *around the waist in a desperate attempt to keep her close to her.)* Let go of me! Marley! Let— go—of—me! *(After a brief struggle she undoes* MARLEY'S *arms from around her waist, then shoves her to the floor. After a moment, she picks up the suitcase, opens it, and dumps everything out onto the floor. She looks at* MARLEY.) This is my suitcase, by the way! *(She goes to the bedroom. Slams shut the door.* MARLEY *is still on the floor. Sobbing. She begins to gather her stuff from all around her. Pause.)*

(STEPH *re-enters the den from the bedroom with her hair tied back, wearing a jean jacket. No suitcase. A large pocketbook over her shoulder.)*

STEPH You know what? Fuck bringing anything from here! I don't want the smell of this house or—or anyone in it close to me. I'm starting out brand-fucking-new! *(She goes to the shelf where the stereo is.)* 'Cept for a few favorite CDs—fuck everythin' else, you can have it all. *(She goes through the CDs. Chooses the ones she wants, puts them in her pocketbook. Stops for a moment. To herself)* You hated Dawn that much, and I didn't know it. How did I not know?

(MARLEY *is still gathering her stuff from the floor.)*

MARLEY *(Through her tears)* If—if Ma killed you last night, I—I would've killed myself, I know it. I'm—uh—*(Breaks down some.)* I'm sorry—if that—if that means anything—

(Pause. STEPH *turns to look down at* MARLEY. *After a beat she bends and picks up a small doll.)*

STEPH Ole Rosey . . .

MARLEY *(Softly)* She's been through everything, too, right?

STEPH I remember getting her outta that car fire over on Elmwood Avenue.

MARLEY Couldn't believe you went back for her.

STEPH She's family . . . even if she is bald.

(Silence.)

MARLEY I—I got a crush on this boy. Name's Peter.

STEPH *(Through her tears)* Is he nerdy smart like you?

MARLEY *(Nods.)* And he just dyed his hair orange.

STEPH Oh, so now he's Peter, Peter the Pumpkin-eater? *(*MARLEY *laughs. Three sharp blasts of a car horn.* STEPH *looks in the direction they came from, then back to* MARLEY. *They lock eyes for a moment. Through her tears)* Is he a nice guy? This Peter?

MARLEY He's—like—too good to be true. *(She turns away from* STEPH *to find her wallet on the floor.* STEPH *kisses the doll and puts it down, then removes one of her favorite CDs, which she puts next to the stereo. She looks at* MARLEY *one last time, then exits.* MARLEY *removes the photo of Peter from her wallet.)* Huge eyes . . . *(She stands, then turns to where* STEPH *was.)* Like chestnuts . . . *(She stands frozen, looking into the emptiness as music comes up softly for a few beats. Then the lights begin a slow fade to black.)*

War

> BILL BOZZONE

'99

ORIGINAL PRODUCTION

DIRECTOR Christine Farrell
SET DESIGNER Carlo Adinolfi
COSTUME DESIGNER Austin Sanderson
SOUND Robert Gould
PROPS Erika Malone
PRODUCTION STAGE MANAGER Gail Eve Malatesta
STAGE MANAGER Jonathan Donahue

The cast was as follows:
JIMMY Corey Behnke
PAULINE Sylva Kelegian
VITO Gary Wolf

CHARACTERS

VITO eighteen, a high-school senior about to graduate
PAULINE thirty-six, his mother
JIMMY eighteen, Vito's friend and "co-conspirator"

PLACE

Bay Ridge, Brooklyn, circa 1966

TIME

Memorial Day, around 11:30 a.m.

A fairly large "eat-in" kitchen with the standard appliances. A front door, or the suggestion of one. An exit/entrance into the rest of the house. A Formica table covered with a checkered tablecloth, wooden chairs painted black, cabinets above the stove and below the sink. Drawers next to the sink. On the stove, a pot of coffee. Above the stove, perhaps on a shelf, a ceramic teapot. Mounted on the wall, a rotary phone. On one of the chairs, a backpack.

PAULINE CHRISTIANNI *sits in one of the chairs. Dressed in summer shorts and a blouse, she removes a pair of sandals. Close by, on the seat of one of the other chairs, a box from Macy's.* VITO *hovers close by. He's dressed in a robe and slippers.*

VITO Please?

PAULINE Forget it, Vee. Driving around with a learner's permit, no
   licensed driver in the car . . .

VITO There'll be a licensed driver. That's what I'm trying to tell
   you. Jimmy DeFelice is going to be with me.

PAULINE Sorry, buddy-boy.

VITO Ma, come on. A chance to see Dick Weber. He's probably never going to be through this way again.

PAULINE Can't you just watch him on TV?

VITO It's not the same.

PAULINE *(To herself)* All this fuss over some bowler.

VITO Not just "some bowler," Ma. Four-time U.S. Open bowling champion.

PAULINE So how come you can't take the bus?

VITO Because it's St. Nick's. It's not even close to a bus.

PAULINE I'll pick up the paper, I'll read about my son being another holiday statistic. *(Short pause.)* Besides, I want you here when Charles arrives.

VITO For what?

PAULINE For never mind.

VITO Tell you what, you lend me the car, I'll stick around.

PAULINE Oh, so you make the rules now.

VITO Ma, come on. Please.

PAULINE *(After a moment.)* Let me think about it.

VITO Jimmy's probably on his way over right now.

PAULINE I said let me think about it. (VITO, *dejected, walks to the table and sits. Off, the sounds of a marching band tuning up. A bass drum is struck, some men laugh, a car horn is heard.)* Listen to that racket. *(She stands.)* Every Memorial Day the same thing. *(She goes for the Macy's box.)* Next they'll be staggering down Ocean Avenue. Waving their banners. "We Support Our Troops in Vietnam." The murder of innocent women and kids is what they support. *(She begins to remove her shorts.)*

VITO They like to remember. It's no different than you with those stupid old records.

PAULINE Hey. Don't be fresh. *(Beat.)* Besides, it's a lot different.

Those records give me memories of your father. *(VITO looks over at his mother, who is now in blouse and panties. PAULINE aware of the look she's getting, looks over at him. Slight smile.)* What?

VITO *(Looks away.)* Nothing.

PAULINE You'd think people'd know better by now. My God, 1966 and we're still slaughtering each other like barbarians. *(Pause.)* Eat some breakfast before you go anywhere. *(She takes a miniskirt from the Macy's box, begins to put it on. VITO gets a carton of milk, a bowl and spoon, some cereal. He brings them to the table.)* I thought you didn't like Jimmy DeFelice.

VITO He's all right.

PAULINE Last year he was "the kootie."

VITO Well, now he's got a driver's license.

PAULINE You gonna have time to pick up your tux for tomorrow night?

VITO I'm not going.

PAULINE Vito, please. I got enough on my mind.

VITO I'm serious. I don't want to go.

PAULINE Your senior prom. You have to go.

VITO I was thinking maybe you and me could do something.

PAULINE Oh yeah? Like what?

VITO Like anything. We could go out and get something to eat or something.

PAULINE *(After a moment.)* Did you at least call Linda?

VITO Yesss . . .

PAULINE Because I don't want her mother down my back.

VITO It's all taken care of.

(PAULINE, in the miniskirt, stands in front of VITO.)

PAULINE So what's the verdict? *(She does a turn.)* I saw it at Macy's yesterday, I thought it was kinda summery.

VITO It's a little short.

PAULINE It's a miniskirt. It's supposed to be short.

VITO They'll let you wear that at work?

PAULINE I didn't get it for work. I got it for play. I figured I'd take it with me down to D.C.

VITO Today?

PAULINE Of course today. When else?

VITO It's just very sexy. That's all.

(PAULINE, *flattered by this, smiles.*)

PAULINE Vito!

VITO You know what I mean. It's too young for you.

PAULINE That's not what you said the first time. You said "sexy."

VITO I just don't want people to get the wrong idea.

(PAULINE *starts toward the sink.*)

PAULINE Like who?

VITO Like Charlie Tuna, that's like who.

PAULINE Hey. Charles *Turner* puts food on that table. If I was you, I would not bite the hand. *(She takes down the teapot, opens the lid, takes out some cash, returns the teapot.)*

VITO Ma, come on. The guy's a big phony. You ever listen to the way he talks?

(PAULINE *takes the cash to the backpack, unzips it, puts the cash in her wallet, rezips.*)

PAULINE It's called educated.

VITO He's my age.

PAULINE He's twenty-six, Vee. That's not quite eighteen.

VITO Closer to me than you. *(Pause.)* I just don't get why you have to go to D.C. with him.

PAULINE *(Approaches.)* We've been through this, Vee. It's a war protest. There's gonna be hundreds of people there.

(VITO *drops the spoon in the bowl, stands.*)

VITO So what do they need you for?

PAULINE Strength in numbers. Besides, you can't end a war by sitting at home on your hands.

VITO I'm not stupid, you know. (VITO *takes the bowl to the sink.*) Two people go away for a weekend, a little more than protesting takes place.

PAULINE Hey, Charles hates this war as much as I do. More people like him in this world, maybe we won't have to turn on the TV every night and watch some poor GI with his legs blown off. (*Pause.*) Besides, if it wasn't for Charles, I'd still be behind a teller's cage making $96 a week. I would not be assistant vice president of new accounts.

VITO Big deal.

PAULINE You'll change your tune.

VITO What's that supposed to mean?

(PAULINE *approaches, stops, smiles.*)

PAULINE Okay, it's supposed to be Charles's surprise, but I'll let you in on it. This isn't a for-sure thing, Vee. But it's an almost-for-sure thing. (*Beat.*) Charles thinks he can get you into Kingsborough Community College for the fall.

VITO Ma . . .

PAULINE I know what you're gonna say. You didn't exactly burn down Holy Trinity with your grades. But Charles knows the head of the accounting department.

VITO Accounting?

PAULINE It's a real foot up in the banking business.

VITO I don't want to go into the banking business.

PAULINE Just talk to him when he gets here. Will you do that?

VITO I don't take favors, Ma. Not from people like Charlie Tuna. (*Beat.*) And you shouldn't either. I know exactly what guys like him are after, and it has nothing to do with accounting.

PAULINE *(Short pause.)* I don't believe this. You're jealous.

VITO Am not.

PAULINE I think it's cute. My little bulldog protecting his turf. *(The telephone rings.* PAULINE, *closest to the phone, picks it up. Into phone)* Hello? *(She listens.)* Oh hiya, Rosemary. What's up? *(This gets* VITO'*s attention. After a moment, into phone)* No, he's standing right here . . .

VITO *(Indicating off.)* I'm gonna go—

*(*PAULINE *holds up a hand for* VITO *to remain right where he is.)*

PAULINE *(Into phone)* No, he didn't tell me . . . *(She looks over at* VITO *as she listens.)* Uh-huh . . . Why would she do that? . . . Uh-huh . . . No offense, Rosemary, but isn't that kinda a low-class thing to do? . . . I'm not *saying* I blame you. I'm just saying I'm surprised that Linda would . . . No, no, you're right. You can't murder the messenger. *(She shakes her head.)* Tomorrow? Actually, I'll miss Mass tomorrow, but I should be back in time for Sweet Adelines . . . Good, I'll talk to you then. *(She hangs up the phone. Pause.)* Why do you keep me in the dark all the time?

VITO Ma, please. It's no big thing.

PAULINE According to Linda's mother, it *is* a big thing. According to Linda's mother, Linda decided to go to the prom with somebody else.

VITO Can we talk about this some other time?

PAULINE No, we cannot. *(Pause.)* You still got the ticket?

VITO Somewhere.

PAULINE Good. Because you're going to that thing.

VITO By myself?

PAULINE You won't be by yourself. Not for long.

VITO Ma. Really. It's nothing. *(He goes to one of the drawers next to the sink, begins rummaging through it.)*

PAULINE What are you looking for?

VITO My birth certificate. I got to renew my learner's permit.

PAULINE You can't show 'em the old one?

VITO I need two forms of I.D.

PAULINE *(Approaches.)* Here. Let me look. *(She looks through the drawers.)* So what's his name? *(No response.)* The boy Linda dropped you for. What's his name?

VITO Jack Baggs. You don't know him. *(Indicates entrance/exit.)* Look, can I just—

PAULINE Not if you want the car you can't.

(Pause.)

VITO You're going to let me have the car?

PAULINE If you cooperate. If you're nice. *(She finds a candy tin, takes it from the drawer, carries it to the table.)* Get your mother a cup of coffee.

(VITO sighs, goes to the stove, pours the coffee.)

VITO So what do I have to do?

(PAULINE begins to remove the miniskirt, puts her shorts and sandals back on.)

PAULINE Listen to what I tell you. It'll take about ten minutes. Charles should be here by then, you two can talk. I'll go out to the garage and finish painting protest signs.

VITO And then I get the car?

PAULINE Then you get the car. *(Pause.)* So. Why would Linda choose somebody like Jack Baggs over you?

VITO I don't know. He's just a cooler guy, I guess.

PAULINE *(Beat.)* I like that answer. *(She sits, opens the candy tin, begins to thumb through.)* He's not better-looking, he's not smarter, he's simply "a cooler guy."

VITO He's also better-looking and smarter.

PAULINE *(Looks up.)* I don't believe that. You know why? *(No re-*

sponse.) Because you have your mother's looks and your father's brains, and there's not a man God breathed life into that can compete with that. *(Beat.)* "Cool," fortunately, is something that can be taught. *(She again begins to thumb through the candy tin.)* Get the record player from my bedroom. And my records.

VITO Right now?

PAULINE No. Next week. (VITO *sighs, exits. She continues to thumb through documents in the tin. In a moment,* VITO *reenters with a record player and a stack of 78 rpm records. He goes to one of the cabinets under the sink, finds an extension cord, sets up the record player after removing the tablecloth.)* The whole key, Vito, is this. A woman is powerless in the presence of a truly confident man. *(Pause.)* Your father and me. The perfect example.

VITO You said ten minutes, Ma.

PAULINE *(Ignoring him.)* We were living on Avenue X at the time. Grandma, myself, and Aunt Bridget, who was carrying your cousin Maureen . . .

VITO *(Indicates refrigerator.)* You mind if I have a beer?

PAULINE No beer. *(Beat.)* Your father had just started driving for Neptune Laundry Service. The dirty-diaper man we used to call him. *(Beat. She smiles.)* First time he saw me sunning myself in the driveway, you know what he said?

VITO He said, "Ninety-two degrees just got a whole lot hotter."

PAULINE I told you this?

VITO He saw you in the driveway, he asked you out, you turned him down.

PAULINE Because he drove a laundry truck. What kind of future is that? Besides, I had my own career to pursue. Back then people told me I had a better voice than—

VITO —Peggy Lee. I know.

(PAULINE *looks through the records.)*

PAULINE Still, he kept at it. Refused to take no for an answer. That's confidence, Vee. A woman reacts to that. *(She hands* VITO *a record.)* Here. Put this on. *(*VITO *sighs, puts on the record. Kay Starr sings "Wheel of Fortune.")* We're gonna pretend. I'm gonna show you how certain things are done between a man and a woman.

VITO Do we really have to?

PAULINE Okay. We're at the prom. Jack Baggs has gone off some-place, probably to compare knives with his juvenile delinquent friends. *(She pulls out a chair.)* Linda is all by herself, already sorry that she didn't come with you. *(She sits, folds her hands in her lap, looks up at* VITO. *After a moment.)* I doubt, Vee, that she has all night for this.

VITO *(Beat.)* I don't know. I guess I would go up, I'd ask her to dance, she'd say no, I'd come home and maybe watch television. *(Pause.)*

PAULINE Okay, now this time don't tell me. Show me. *(*VITO *hesitates.)* Vee, that car is not rolling out of the driveway unless you make a serious effort.

VITO *(Sighs, approaches.)* You wanna dance?

*(*PAULINE *looks up at* VITO, *smiles.)*

PAULINE No thank you.

VITO *(Shrugs.)* I didn't think so.

(Pause. PAULINE *stands, removes the needle from the record.)*

PAULINE Damn it, Vito, that was so half-assed it breaks my heart.

VITO The girl says no, she says no.

PAULINE But she doesn't *mean* no. Don't you get it? When a girl says no, she's just telling you she needs more encouragement.

VITO The car has gas in it?

PAULINE Will you forget the car for one second? *(She indicates the chair.)* Here. You be Linda.

VITO Ma . . .

PAULINE I'll be you. Sit. (VITO *sighs, hesitates, sits.* PAULINE *approaches him, smiles.*) Good evening, Linda. How are you tonight?

VITO Fine.

PAULINE As fine as you look?

VITO God, Ma . . .

PAULINE I was studying you from across the room and I got this vision. You and me. And we're gliding across the dance floor like ice skaters. And I was just wondering if you might help me complete the picture.

VITO Sorry, I've got my period. (*He smiles.*)

PAULINE (*After a moment, as herself*) Are we gonna be serious about this, or are you gonna crack jokes?

VITO I was just—

PAULINE Stand up. (*Pause.* VITO *gets to his feet.*) Because this is what Linda'd be doing at this point. Standing up and accompanying you onto the dance floor. (*She puts the record back on, turns, assumes slow-dance position.*) I'll lead. (VITO *takes his mother's hand, puts his other hand on her back, moves with her to the music.*) Okay. It now becomes your responsibility to make conversation.

VITO Like what?

PAULINE Like try asking her interests.

VITO What are your interests?

PAULINE (*As a girl*) I enjoy music, dancing, and church-related activities. Yourself?

VITO I like watching TV and bowling.

PAULINE My. You must be awful strong to be able to lift those heavy balls.

VITO She would never say that, Ma.

PAULINE (*As herself*) How do you know?

VITO No girl would ever say that.

PAULINE You don't know *what* she's gonna say, Vee. That's the point. For every action, you gotta have a reaction. *(Pause. They continue to dance. As the girl)* So, Vito. Do you enjoy taking walks?

VITO Walks?

PAULINE The stars are out, it's warm . . .

VITO What if it's raining?

PAULINE We can find cover somewhere.

(They dance.)

VITO *(After a moment.)* So would you like to take a walk or something?

(PAULINE stops dancing, stares at Vito.)

PAULINE Let me get my coat. *(Pause. She smiles. As herself)* That was excellent, Vee. The way you picked up on her cue. She wanted to be alone with you, and that lightbulb over your head finally went on.

VITO That's it?

PAULINE Of course that's not "it." That's not the half of it. *(She takes the needle from the record.)* You've taken this girl outside, you've gone for a walk, you've ended up—let's say, in the park on the grass somewhere. *(Beat.)* Now what do you do?

VITO I don't know.

PAULINE Well, you can't just stand there. Suppose there's no benches? *(Pause.)* See now, this is where the blanket comes in handy.

VITO What blanket?

PAULINE The blanket. You always bring a blanket.

VITO Isn't that going to look kind of stupid?

PAULINE Well, you don't carry it out in the open, you hide it. You maybe stick it in a gym bag and check it at the door. *(She takes* *the folded tablecloth, hands it to* VITO.*)* Here. Spread it out. *(*VITO *hesitates, then spreads it on the floor.* PAULINE *takes a seat, looks up at* VITO, *smiles, pats the area next to herself.* VITO *finally sits next to her.)* Good. *(Beat.)* At this point, Vee, the girl is gonna wanna open up to you. All you need to do is nod your head and listen.

VITO Okay.

PAULINE *(Beat. As the girl)* Can I tell you a secret? *(No response. As herself)* Nod your head. *(*VITO *does. As the girl)* My parents don't understand me. *(*VITO *nods.)* They treat me like a kid. They have no idea of the woman I've started to become. *(Pause.)* What about your parents?

VITO What about them?

PAULINE *(As herself)* Vito, come on. You're making progress. Don't drop the ball now.

VITO *(After a moment.)* There's only my mother. My father died when I was three.

PAULINE *(As the girl)* Oh, my. How did that happen?

VITO You know. The Korean thing.

PAULINE *(As herself)* Korean *War*, Vito. Call it what it was.

VITO Korean War.

PAULINE Your poor mom. *(She moves closer to* VITO, *rests a hand on his knee.)* Left widowed and so young.

VITO I guess.

*(*PAULINE *lightly brushes his hair with her hand.)*

PAULINE Do you love her?

VITO Ma . . .

*(*PAULINE *lets her hand rest on* VITO's *cheek.)*

PAULINE *(Smiles.)* Well, do you?

VITO *(After a moment.)* I guess.

PAULINE I imagine she must—*(A knock at the front door. As herself)*

Oh, jeez. That must be Charles. *(She stands, starts for the door.)* Fold up the tablecloth, Vee. We don't want the man thinking we've just escaped from Bellevue. *(*VITO *folds the tablecloth.* PAULINE *answers the door.* JIMMY *stands in the doorway.)*

JIMMY Hi, Mrs. Christianni.

PAULINE Jimmy. Excuse me. I was expecting somebody else.

JIMMY Vito around?

VITO In here, Jimmy.

*(*JIMMY *enters. He's a kid around* VITO's *age, slight of build, easily picked on.)*

JIMMY You ready?

VITO I gotta wait for my mother's boyfriend.

JIMMY I could sit in the car and listen to the radio.

PAULINE You don't have to do that, Jimmy. *(Indicates chair.)* Here. You have breakfast?

JIMMY I wouldn't mind a cup of coffee.

*(*JIMMY *sits.* PAULINE *goes to the stove, pours* JIMMY *a cup.* VITO *approaches* PAULINE, *holds his hand out.)*

PAULINE What?

VITO Keys? *(*PAULINE *reluctantly reaches into her pocket, takes out a set of car keys, hands it to* VITO. *To* JIMMY*)* I'll be right back. I'm just gonna change. *(He exits.* PAULINE *gives* JIMMY *his coffee, takes a seat across from him, begins to look through the candy tin.)*

PAULINE So, Jimmy. You set for the prom?

JIMMY Not going.

PAULINE Handsome boy like you, why not?

JIMMY *(Shrugs.)* Rather hang out with Vito.

PAULINE Vito's going.

JIMMY With who?

PAULINE Linda Murphy.

JIMMY That skank?

PAULINE She's a nice girl. Why do you say that?

JIMMY Are you kidding? Her and Vito got into it like World War III. Right there in homeroom. Linda's talking all this bullcrap about peaceful co-existence, old Vee stands up and lets her have it good.

(PAULINE looks over at this.)

PAULINE He didn't tell me this.

JIMMY You'd have been proud of him, Mrs. Christianni. He blew her doors off. Told old Linda she'd change her opinion if *her* father'd been blown to smithereens. *(PAULINE freezes. JIMMY approaches.)* Whatcha looking for? *(No response.)* Mrs. Christianni? *(PAULINE looks up at JIMMY.)* Maybe I can help. Whatcha looking for? *(JIMMY rises, crosses behind PAULINE.)*

PAULINE Nothing. Vito's birth certificate.

JIMMY *(After a moment.)* You mean he told you? *(Pause. Slight laugh.)* That little peckerhead. He makes me swear not to say a word, and here he already told you. *(He reaches forward, grabs a bunch of documents from the tin, and begins to look through them.)*

PAULINE Jimmy, is this something about the car?

JIMMY Well, it's hard to get there without the car. It's all the way down in Fort Hamilton. *(JIMMY pulls out a document.)* Here it is.

PAULINE What's down in Fort Hamilton?

JIMMY The recruiting office. *(Calls off)* Hey, Vito! I found your birth certificate! *(To PAULINE)* They won't even *talk* to you without a birth certificate. *(He puts the document on the table.)*

PAULINE Vito didn't say anything about a recruiting office.

JIMMY He didn't?

PAULINE He said you were gonna go watch somebody bowl.

JIMMY *(Beat.)* Oh. *(Beat.)* Yeah, well, we might do that, too.

(PAULINE *rises, starts away.*) See, I thought he already . . . (*Pause.*) It's pretty safe now, Mrs. Christianni, really. The army's even got something called the Buddy System. You enlist with a friend, they keep you together. That way you always have somebody watching your back. (*Pause.*) Mrs. Christianni?

PAULINE I think you should leave now, Jimmy.

JIMMY But we're supposed to—

PAULINE Not today.

(JIMMY *starts for the door, stops.*)

JIMMY (*After a moment.*) Would you tell Vito to call me? (*No response.*) Mrs. Christianni? (*No response. He moves to the door.*) Thanks for the coffee.

(*He hesitates, exits,* PAULINE *moves to the table, sees the birth certificate, picks it up. She glances around the room.*)

VITO (*Off. Calls*) Hey, Jimmy. (PAULINE *moves to the sink, sticks the birth certificate inside the teapot.*) Maybe you could go out and check the oil while I—(*He reenters, looks around.*) Where's Jimmy?

PAULINE Gone.

VITO What do you mean "gone"?

PAULINE He forgot something.

VITO But he'll be right back.

PAULINE (*Beat. Looks over.*) He'll be right back.

VITO (*Beat.*) So where's my birth certificate?

PAULINE I put it away.

VITO What did you do that for? (*No response. He goes to the candy tin.*)

PAULINE You won't find it in there, Vee. I hid it.

VITO (*Beat. Faces her.*) For what?

PAULINE I just don't want you running out of here before we finish our lesson.

VITO Ma . . .

PAULINE Finish the lesson, I'll give you your birth certificate. *(She moves to the table.)*

VITO This is so stupid.

*(*PAULINE *pushes two of the chairs together.)*

PAULINE Now then. You've danced, you've talked, you take her home. Linda, at this point, will probably suggest you both sit on the porch swing before she goes inside.

VITO Linda doesn't have a porch swing.

PAULINE Her front steps, then. *(She sits in one of the chairs.)* Like it or not, you're gonna have to kiss this girl, Vee.

VITO Ma . . .

PAULINE She's expecting it and I think she's more than entitled. *(Pause.)*

VITO Two minutes. *(He sits.)*

PAULINE Okay, now show me your move.

VITO My what?

PAULINE Your "move," Vito. The way in which you plan to make physical contact.

VITO *(Beat.)* I don't know, Ma . . . I guess I would . . .

(He hesitates, yawns, and stretches. His arm winds up across the back of PAULINE*'s chair.* PAULINE *looks over at him.)*

PAULINE *(Beat.)* That's not bad.

VITO I saw it on TV.

PAULINE It's not bad. *(Pause.)* Now what?

VITO Now I guess—

PAULINE Show me.

*(*VITO *hesitates, moves in.* PAULINE *faces him. They kiss, lip-to-lip. In a moment, they separate.)*

VITO *(After a moment.)* We done?

PAULINE Just one more thing. *(Pause.)* You're out on the porch, you're sitting, she might say something like . . . *(As the girl)* Gee, Vito, it sure has gotten chilly. *(Pause. As herself)* See, now that's a cue, buddy-boy. That's where you reach for your blanket . . . . *(She takes the tablecloth.)* . . . and you put it around the two of you like this. *(Silence. She rests her head on* VITO's *shoulder. After a moment.)* And then she might say, Stay with me, Vito.

VITO Why would she say that, Ma?

PAULINE Because she doesn't want you to go.

(Pause. At this point military music, hardly discernible, is heard. It should have the definite sound of an amateur high-school band.)

VITO He told you, didn't he? *(No response. To himself)* Goddamn it, Jimmy . . . *(He rises, walks away.)*

PAULINE What were you gonna do, Vito? Just take off without saying anything?

VITO I need my birth certificate.

(He begins to search. PAULINE *is on her feet.)*

PAULINE Your father at least told me. Your father at least had the guts to sit me down and lie to me and say things'd be all right.

VITO Where is it?

PAULINE You know how much I hate this fucking war!

VITO *(Stops searching, faces her.)* Well, I don't! *(Pause.)* It's exciting, Ma. That's a word I don't hear very much in this neighborhood! It's a word I'll *never* hear if I'm trapped in some stupid job married to Linda Murphy the rest of my life!

PAULINE And what am I supposed to do? *(No response.)* I'll tell you what I *will* do. I'll sit here and I'll wait and I won't buy a newspaper or turn on the radio. The phone'll ring, people'll knock, but I won't answer. I'll drop the mail on the table without even looking at it. *(Beat.)* But it won't do me any good, Vee. Because disaster always finds a way in. It tells you how brave your man was. How we all make sacrifices. How he died a "good" death. And it's a lie, Vito. You'll find that out. It's the biggest lie ever told!

VITO Tell me where my birth certificate is. *(No response.)* Please, Ma. *(No response.)* Goddamn it!

(He returns to searching. Things are overturned, flipped through, discarded. PAULINE approaches.)

PAULINE Vito, listen to me. Eventually Charles is gonna move on. I know that. He's gonna meet a younger woman and poof. But it's not gonna matter. Because there's you. And I can make you happy, Vee, I swear to God I can.

(VITO accidentally nudges the teapot, which falls to the floor and breaks. He sees the birth certificate, bends, picks it up. The two face each other.)

VITO I hafta go.

PAULINE Vito . . . *(VITO stops, faces his mother.)* I see the way you look at me sometimes. Like before. And I know what you're thinking, and it's all right. It's the same way your father used to look at me.

(Pause.)

VITO You're just like the Communists. *(Beat.)* They go out into the jungle, they dig a twenty-foot trench, they line the sides with broken glass. You fall into one of those things and you either cut yourself to shreds or go crazy waiting for help.

PAULINE Please don't do this to me.

(VITO starts for the door, stops, faces PAULINE.)

VITO *(After a moment.)* I'm not him, Ma.

PAULINE I know, but you're so damn close. *(Pause. Then VITO turns and quickly exits.)* Vee? *(Pause.)* Vito Christianni, you get back in here right now!

(The military music, which has been swelling since we first heard it, is more noticeable now. PAULINE *goes to the broken teapot, sweeps the pieces into a dustpan, dumps them. The music continues to get louder.* PAULINE *goes to the table, studies the record player. She moves the needle to the record, sits. Kay Starr sings "Wheel of Fortune." Eventually the military music is all that can be heard as the lights fade.)*

The Once Attractive Woman

›CHRISTINE FARRELL

'99

ORIGINAL PRODUCTION

DIRECTOR Eliza Beckwith

ASSISTANT DIRECTOR Paul Hunter

SET DESIGNER Carlo Adinolfi

COSTUME DESIGNER Austin Sanderson

SOUND Robert Gould

FIGHT DIRECTOR Ian Marshall

PROPS Erika Malone

PRODUCTION STAGE MANAGER Gail Eve Malatesta

STAGE MANAGER Paul Powell

The cast was as follows:

ANNE Barrie Youngfellow

PETER/MICK Chris Lutkin

DULCI Debbie Lee Jones

LILY Saundra McClain

HUSBAND Ted Neustadt

CHARACTERS

ANNE fifty, poetry professor at a university

HUSBAND fifty, dry sense of humor, physically strong man

PETER forty, shy computer professor

MICK thirty, adjunct professor from Belfast

PETER and **MICK** can be played by the same actor

DULCI late forties, administrative assistant in English Department

LILY fifties, African-American literature professor at the university; a strong black woman

NOTE

The original design was very fluid. There were chairs on wheels surrounding the stage that were rolled on and off quickly for scene changes. A real basketball was used, a desk on wheels for the office scene, and gym mats for the wrestling scene. The lights never went to black, and rock music was used to aid the transitions.

"What is the fate of a woman who is truly spontaneously alive,
Who is rooted in her body like a redwood in the earth,
Who is in command of startling sexuality that infuses everything."

—ROSEANNE CASH on Patsy Cline

SCENE ONE

ANNE *and* PETER *sit in a car.* ANNE *is driving. They sit far apart throughout the scene. There is sexual tension in the scene.*

PETER Your poetry worked well tonight.

ANNE Your computer design held it up.

PETER It was a great project.

ANNE Your students loved it.

PETER Two classes working together was a challenge.

ANNE Yeah . . . So it's over.

PETER It was a lot of work.

ANNE Poetry and computers . . . hah . . . university style. We worked well together.

PETER We were hot. *(Major pregnant pause.)* Drop me off wherever.

ANNE Preferably your house . . . I mean . . .

PETER Whatever.

ANNE Don't look at me like that.

PETER I'm not, I won't . . . I'll try. *(He takes a deep breath, squirms in his seat.)*

ANNE *(She breathes heavily, tries not to look at him.)* All right . . . Okay . . . I could take you right here and ride you till next Nicklemas!

PETER You didn't say that. I didn't hear that.

ANNE I am beside myself . . . didn't say that.

PETER I didn't hear that.

ANNE I'm a married woman.

PETER I heard that . . . Ride me to Nicklemas . . . Let me out at the corner.

ANNE I love my husband. I really love my husband.

PETER I even love your husband.

ANNE I have children.

PETER I don't like children.

ANNE I love my kids.

PETER I don't know your kids, but I'm sure I'd like them.

ANNE You would, you would.

PETER Let me out of the car!!

ANNE I have to stop the car!

(She stops the car and he gets out. The final beat of the scene is like the af-terglow of a cigarette.)

PETER I'm out of the car.

ANNE I'm not getting out of the car.

PETER Right. I could lean in and kiss you . . . once.

ANNE With your body outside of the car.

(They kiss.)

PETER Good night, attractive woman.

ANNE You're a saint martyred in your middle age, Dr. Sorenson.
   (He leaves; she is looking in the car mirror, talking to herself.) Attractive woman . . . "You could see she was once an attractive
   woman." The once-attractive-woman-in-her-forties literary
   genre. Once, as in one time only, one time in the past for-
   merly. Why not "once and for all" attractive . . . or finally, at
   any time an attractive woman. When does the "once" happen to
   you?

(Blackout. ANNE *removes jacket in blackout and is wearing sweats underneath.)*

SCENE TWO

In this scene ANNE *and a younger man are playing basketball. The same actor from the last scene has changed and plays the Irish teaching assistant.*

MICK You're not bad, for a tenured professor.

ANNE It's my ball. Winner take it out.

MICK Forget it. I'll be late for class. I've got to teach two sections.

ANNE No. Give me the ball. We're playing to twenty-one. I need
   two points. I could beat you. You can't stop.

MICK You're ancient and you're a woman. Trust me. Forget it.

ANNE I'm going to kick your ignorant apathetic ass, Irish boy.

MICK You couldn't beat me if I was wearing a kilt and playing the bagpipes.

(They fight over the ball.)

ANNE We're playing to twenty-one. Give me that ball.

(He's hugging the ball with both hands. He turns away. She pinches his ass. He yelps and turns. She grabs the ball and starts dribbling.)

MICK Owwww . . . What is your problem, Anne?

ANNE Give it up, you little whining teaching assistant. The ball is in play.

(He's guarding her, she can't get around him.)

MICK You think you're tough. You're challenging me.

ANNE No, doofus, I'm going to beat you.

MICK We should make love.

ANNE Oh my God. That's supposed to distract me.

MICK It would be fun. A romp.

ANNE A "romp." What is that, a Celtic term?

MICK Concentrate on the ball now, older lady. Get around me. Go ahead.

ANNE You couldn't dream the sex I've had, younger man. *(She grabs his shorts and snaps them and tries to get around.)*

MICK Oh, please. Is this the sixties lecture?

ANNE You're gonna lose.

MICK You're beside yourself. It's over.

(He grabs the back of her shirt, she is trying to dribble forward and can't.)

ANNE Let me go, no fair . . . no fair.

(She dribbles backward, grabs his shorts, and pulls them down. He lets go. She jumps to take her shot, and he grabs her shorts and pulls them down.)

ANNE Oh Jeez . . . what the hell . . .

(They pull up their shorts, embarrassed and looking around.)

MICK You've been looking for trouble for weeks . . . I'd be up for it. Think about it. *(He exits.)*

ANNE *(Knowing he can't hear her)* What was that? I am beside myself . . . I've got to teach at four o'clock. *(She grabs her suit jacket and purse and runs to the office area.)*

SCENE THREE

ANNE *rushes into an office area,* DULCI *is at the desk and* LILY *is standing reading something. During the scene,* ANNE *puts on her suit jacket.*

ANNE Do I look flushed? *(She takes off her sneakers and sweats and puts on a skirt and heels to go with the suit jacket while she talks.)*

DULCI Yeah.

LILY You look excited. You okay?

ANNE Oh my . . . God . . . Do I . . . I . . . Well . . . my teaching assistant . . .

DULCI Mick Kelly?

LILY He got you excited?

ANNE Sort of, well . . . flushed.

DULCI Close the door.

ANNE It was nothing. He just . . . Never mind.

DULCI He just . . . what?

ANNE Promise you will not repeat this.

LILY I have too much to say to repeat anything.

DULCI Cross my heart.

ANNE He said . . . we should make love.

DULCI The teaching assistant from Belfast . . . He's always at the gym.

ANNE What do you think he meant?

LILY That is not Middle English, Anne. What about that don't you understand?

DULCI The healthy guy, right?

ANNE I'm losing it.

DULCI What happened?

ANNE Nothing happened.

LILY Everything happened.

ANNE In my mind's eye. I guess . . .

DULCI You can't fool around, your husband is like . . .

ANNE Last week something happened.

DULCI Before this . . . what . . . Where were you?

ANNE I kissed the computer professor last week.

DULCI Where did you do that?

ANNE In my car. I was driving him home after the project.

DULCI This is unfair. These things should happen to me. I'm single. You need to throw some cold water on yourself.

LILY *(To* DULCI*)* You need to widen your range, honey.

ANNE Lily, my daydreams are hair-raising.

LILY Hair-raising . . . God—erotic. Let your erotic side rule . . . It's there for a reason.

ANNE Yeah, it's fun to be a player again.

DULCI Well, I'm not playing anymore. I give up.

ANNE You shouldn't do that to yourself.

DULCI I'm not doing anything to myself. There are very few men available, and the work you have to do to attract them is bullshit.

LILY Life without the erotic . . . The uptight-maiden-aunt literary genre.

DULCI I've got lots of men friends.

LILY Do you daydream about touching them?

DULCI I don't want to talk about this.

ANNE I've got to . . . I can't go to class like this . . . Is this the change or whatever they call it?

LILY The change . . . *(She laughs.)* I hate these words . . . Menopause . . . what an ugly turn of phrase. It has no poetry. Don't use it, Anne.

ANNE Some research scientist named it before he hit puberty.

LILY I call it Fertility Freedom Phase . . . entrance into better sex, deeper wisdom, personal power.

(They laugh.)

ANNE So I kissed the computer guy because I was having a mythological passage.

LILY You kissed the computer guy because you wanted to. Because you want to be a goddess.

ANNE I want what I want when I want it, lately. That's goddess-like.

DULCI I want to be a goddess. I don't want to be a maiden aunt.

ANNE You deserve a sex life, Dulce.

DULCI Can I have one of those guys?

ANNE I have no plans. I'm only daydreaming.

LILY Aren't we nice, and don't we smell like strawberries. Make something happen. You're both gutless.

ANNE Maybe I could talk to them and see if they're interested.

LILY Nooo! Smell them, taste them . . . make a move. Use your God-given instincts, ladies.

ANNE I've never made the first move.

DULCI Me neither. Old-fashioned.

LILY What kind of sex lives do you have?

ANNE Good actually, but I'm married, so . . .

DULCI Don't ask.

LILY Listen to me. Your sexuality has to grow with everything else. You can't leave it in high school or college or even marriage.

ANNE I bet you have a great sex life.

LILY I do.

DULCI You kissed the computer professor. You have a great sex life. And I live in girl-friend land. I feel like I've just been voided at the checkout counter.

LILY You have to do something. At least try to get what you want. Trust me. I've had the best. I had Jim Morrison in his prime, and don't you dare repeat that . . . It's my coolest secret. I'm late for class. Go for it. *(She exits.)*

ANNE I'm dying of embarrassment just thinking about what she said.

DULCI She said she made love to Jim Morrison. She said that . . . right here in my office . . . Like, "I'll have bologna and cheese." I had Jim Morrison in his prime . . .

ANNE You've got to trust a woman who's had Jim Morrison. I got goose bumps . . . I'm out of here.

DULCI Don't leave me like this . . . I'm a mess!

(ANNE comes to center stage and addresses her class, taking papers out of her bag.)

SCENE THREE A

ANNE The Computer Project . . . Impressions? Anyone . . . I thought it was innovative. You experienced the poems in a different way. The Allen Ginsberg graphics—they were hot . . . I mean cool. Peter Sorenson was excited, too . . . I mean pleased with the potential relationship . . . between the disciplines. So . . . we'll see, enough said. Now . . . what's up for today . . .

You'd think by now I'd know my own syllabus. Oh, Emily Dickinson. (*You can see or hear her disappointment.*) She was a recluse by temperament . . . You know, I just can't right now . . . Let's look around here. (*Looks through the book.*) Oh yes . . . yes, let's skip to Anne Sexton . . . you'll get this . . . (*She reads a poem such as Anne Sexton's "The Possessed Witch."*)

SCENE FOUR

ANNE *walks into the next scene. Her husband is portrayed with a comfortable attitude toward her. His movement is minimal; he is relaxing on the couch watching a basketball game. The entire conversation takes place while they both stay involved in the game. The actors should improvise a series of reactions to the game and find emotional release by yelling at the players. The scene ends as the game is tied and goes into sudden death. Often they are watching out of the corner of their eye, but they are not glued to the tube throughout.*

ANNE Kids asleep?

HUSBAND Yup. Both of them.

ANNE Can we have a talk?

HUSBAND Sure.

ANNE I've been thinking about making love to a couple of guys.

HUSBAND Is this going to happen tonight?

ANNE No.

HUSBAND Do I know these guys?

ANNE You know them.

HUSBAND Do they work together?

ANNE I don't want them together. I mean, I think I want them both, but individually. Does that make sense?

HUSBAND You'd like to have an affair . . . no, two different affairs, but you'd like to tell me first.

ANNE Should I be specific?

HUSBAND You're serious. I'm having this . . . a . . . basic reaction . . . after twelve years of marriage . . . What the hell . . . Let's keep a couple of secrets.

ANNE You don't know them well. You just know who they are.

HUSBAND Oh. Yeah. Well . . . *(Pause.)* Anything happen yet?

ANNE Kind of.

HUSBAND Not a good answer. Who are they and have you done more than slow-dance in a public place?

ANNE My teaching assistant and the computer teacher I worked with on the poetry project.

HUSBAND They both thought it would be fun to have sex together.

ANNE With me, not with each other . . . Why would I slow-dance in a public place?

HUSBAND Are these guys waiting outside, or did you tell them you'd get back to them?

ANNE No. I said no.

HUSBAND You're serious. Are we having problems I don't know about?

ANNE No, that's why I said no. I don't want to be with them.

HUSBAND You just want to play with them.

ANNE Maybe.

HUSBAND You want my permission.

ANNE No. Opinion. I'm probably not going to have any more babies, and these forties, they're . . . another kind of passage.

HUSBAND Yeah.

ANNE We said we'd try everything once . . . Maybe it would give me a sense of power or danger or . . .

HUSBAND Uh-huh.

ANNE I wonder if we are just old-fashioned. We were real thinkers in the late sixties. I don't know if this is what I've settled for or what I believe. We used to say we should try everything once.

HUSBAND I tried heroin once. I consider myself lucky.

ANNE We said we weren't going to be like our parents.

HUSBAND Everything would be different. It would change us.

ANNE Have you had anyone else in the past twelve years?

HUSBAND Aha . . . the ultimate trap! I get it. I think I win this round. Yes, it crossed my mind, I've seriously considered it, came close, and I am innocent. I am pure. So you make your own decisions.

ANNE I'm trying.

HUSBAND No, you're not. You want me to help you.

ANNE I'm afraid I'd hurt you.

HUSBAND We've done that a couple of times. Don't you think?

ANNE Yes.

HUSBAND I don't want to know what happens.

ANNE What do you mean, you don't want to know what happens? *(He exits and leaves her staring after him. During this scene* ANNE *has taken off her suit jacket and shoes and gotten comfortable in her sneakers. She is ready for the scene change.)*

SCENE FIVE

ANNE *and* MICK *are chest-passing the basketball back and forth. The power and rhythm of the throw changes with the conversation.*

ANNE I just beat the pants off you.

MICK Yes, you did.

ANNE So where should we go?

MICK Home and alone.

ANNE Because I won.

MICK Because we're friends.

ANNE Oh. You're afraid it will mess everything up.

MICK I know it will mess you up.

ANNE You started this.

MICK No. You did. You pinched my arse.

ANNE You said it out loud.

MICK Your marriage okay?

ANNE *(Visibly upset and embarrassed)* God, you're arrogant! I have a good marriage, you know.

MICK Well, bully for you! So keep it together and stop challenging me . . . I'm not messing it up for someone else.

ANNE I beat you, though.

MICK I didn't put my contacts in and dribbled with my left hand, but you beat me. Don't challenge me again unless you are prepared for the consequences. If you want to play rough or step over the line, there is not going to be anyone around to take care of you afterward.

ANNE Are you lecturing me? *(He exits.)* I'm still your boss, even though I'm humiliated. *(She exits.)*

SCENE SIX

ANNE, LILY, *and* DULCI *enter a workout or warm-up room with a tumbling mat and begin to take off their shoes. A wrestling match takes place in this scene. The* lazzo, *or bit, is that every time the wrestling gets rough, the wrong person gets hit or thrown. They set out to wrestle each other and end up pinning* LILY *to the ground.*

ANNE I already worked out this morning.

DULCI If we do this, Lily is the odd man out.

LILY I'll watch. I'm really sick of your girly-girl exercises.

ANNE This is stupid, it's a man's game.

DULCI You promised. I've played your games and lost miserably.

ANNE I don't know the rules.

LILY Where did you get the idea to wrestle?

DULCI My brother wrestled in high school. We used to fool around. It was fun.

ANNE Men do it in D. H. Lawrence novels. It allows them to embrace.

DULCI We play kids' rules. The first one with their back on the floor for three seconds loses.

ANNE You're nuts.

DULCI I just want to press against something.

ANNE Do they wrestle in black literature?

LILY God, no! Can you imagine Derek Walcott and August Wilson all oiled up. I'd like to see that.

(ANNE *and* DULCI *start circling.*)

ANNE Let's go!

DULCI I've been thinking overtime.

ANNE Yeah.

DULCI Maybe I'll adopt a child.

ANNE Okay.

DULCI Or move to Australia.

LILY Adventure. That's cool.

DULCI Maybe I'll hold eye contact with the guy at the hardware store.

ANNE That's a move. Kind of.

DULCI Thanks to you two, I'm becoming a sex maniac. *(She attacks* ANNE.*)*

ANNE You really haven't had a date in eighteen months?

(They tussle.)

LILY I can't believe that Irish guy said no . . . After all that.

DULCI *(To* ANNE*)* You didn't tell me that.

ANNE It just happened this morning. You want it on the PA system?

*(*DULCI *has her arm around* ANNE*'s neck.)*

DULCI I respect that man. He has a well-developed heart.

*(*ANNE *grabs her leg and pulls her down on the mat.)*

ANNE Oh please . . . He didn't want to do it in the first place.

LILY You started it.

ANNE I hate it.

LILY That's brave.

ANNE It doesn't matter what I wear, men look at me like I'm their mother . . . *(She has her arms around* DULCI*'s back; they are on their knees.)*

LILY He changed his mind. That's fate, Anne.

DULCI Your charisma's dusty . . . *(She lunges and throws* ANNE *over.)* I'm seeing images of my brother.

ANNE You really want to win.

*(*DULCI *has* ANNE*'s leg.)*

DULCI It's clearly desire that counts here.

ANNE You smoke, you hardly work out.

LILY *(She rushes to the mat for the count.)* One . . . two.

DULCI You're frustrated. You couldn't focus on the *Queen Elizabeth II* right now.

ANNE I'm frustrated because I feel invisible! *(She flips over and gets out from under.)* You may be younger, but you are dead meat.

DULCI Focus gives you physical power. *(She is on her knees and* ANNE *grabs her arm and twists it behind her back.)*

ANNE I never beat a man in sports and now it's too late. That stinks!

DULCI Owww, Ow . . . owooooww . . . you're really hurting me. You're gonna break my arm.

(ANNE *releases her.*)

ANNE Sorry, sorry . . . you okay? I'm out of control. Are you all right?

(DULCI *grabs her arm and throws her back down on the mat.*)

DULCI You never beat a man, because your sympathies are in the wrong place. You are going to have to pay for having everything. *(She is holding* ANNE *down.)*

ANNE That's it.

DULCI You've had it.

ANNE How dare you manipulate me.

DULCI Nooooo mercy!

ANNE You're jealous because I have a relationship.

DULCI Wrong again. You're brooding, Meno . . .

ANNE Don't say that M word.

DULCI You're emotional, hot-flash city . . . self-involved.

LILY No. No. Damnit, you are finally involved, listening to your bodies. Look at the two of you. This is erotic. I can taste the adrenaline.

DULCI *Shut up!*

LILY I can't shut up. I've been where you both are. I want to do it! I play the winner.

ANNE I'm not doing this again.

DULCI You're not going to win.

ANNE You're gonna lose . . . you're gonna lose.

LILY Pure physical force. Let your bodies lead. Don't inhibit anything . . . !!

(They stop wrestling and go after LILY, *and all end up on the mat in a pile.)*

ANNE My heart's pounding.

DULCI Let's hear it for D. H. Lawrence and my brother Fred.

ANNE I can't move. We've reached another dimension.

DULCI I wish I'd played a sport in high school. Maybe I'd get over myself.

ANNE I couldn't have gotten through puberty without basketball.

LILY You've got guts . . . What's our next risk?

ANNE Will you stop. She's being really mean and I'm feeling really *aggressive!*

*(*LILY *rolls over and is holding them both.)*

LILY Even if you don't have kids you end up mothering. *(To* ANNE*)* It's darkest before the dawn, honey. *(To* DULCI*)* Now tell me about this guy at the hardware store.

ANNE How come I never noticed you before? In the past three weeks I've begun to hang on your every word. Was I a shallow person before?

LILY You need me. There's nothing wrong with that. You now see me as powerful and sexual, not just older.

ANNE Honestly, I never thought of you as sexual.

LILY It's just like the students. They see us as parents, not people.

DULCI When you said that thing about Jim Morrison that time, you knocked me over. *(Pause.)* His name is Henrick. It's on his shirt.

LILY Eye contact and a touch of his hand.

ANNE Are we going to hear about this great sex life or what?

LILY You don't ask an older woman about her sex life.

ANNE and DULCI We're asking.

LILY I've been in love with the same man for twenty years. We just never wanted to marry. I see other men when the attraction is strong enough. I've had Dr. Fowler in the history department and his wife and they are both lovely. I've had my mythological passage and it's a glorious hell. It's got rhythm and sound and heat. It redesigned my soul. You get dangerous. Embrace it. You couldn't miss it if you tried.

(They are all quiet.)

DULCI I just want to hold someone. Maybe I should choose a woman. I wish I could tell a man what I really want. I usually wait for them to figure it out, they never do. That's when I start judging them. I'm going to tell Henrick he has beautiful eyes.

ANNE I was never going to marry. Then I was never going to have kids—and now.

LILY Everything sneaks up on you and bites you in the heart. You'll figure it out.

ANNE I guess.

DULCI Anne, don't you have your snot-nose class now?

ANNE Yes. I can't be late . . . Jeez . . . I'll have to teach in this. They won't notice . . . To D. H. Lawrence and your brother Fred! *(She moves to the classroom again to talk to the students.)*

SCENE SIX A

ANNE *(To the class as she pulls papers from her bag)* I read your papers . . . unfortunately. It's as if I've had no effect on you this entire semester. Have there been alien pods sitting in those seats? Talk to me. Why aren't you motivated . . . Doesn't the language at least excite something in you? *(She waits for an answer, they all just look at her.)* Listen . . . I'm not mad at you, I'm not failing you . . . I just want to know why you don't hear me. Do you consider the material too old, out-of-date? These writers have a passion that seems universal to me. Many of them are still alive. What? *(She screams out of frustration, to get a rise out of someone.)* It is this smug supercilious gaze that comes over you that I cannot bear. What are your passions . . . Confess or you will not get your precious little A's.

(She turns, walks to center as the light shifts and the HUSBAND *comes on stage and confronts her.)*

SCENE SEVEN

HUSBAND *on stage.* ANNE *enters.*

HUSBAND *(Furious)* Where were you?

ANNE At Mike's basketball game.

HUSBAND Oh, right. You teach till 5:30.

ANNE The game was at 6.

HUSBAND Okay. Where's Mike?

ANNE Putting the balls in the sports closet.

HUSBAND I didn't know where you were.

ANNE You want sweet potatoes?

HUSBAND How dare you?

ANNE Get sweet potatoes?

HUSBAND How dare you talk to me like that? I haven't slept in a week.

ANNE Okay . . . Listen, I was hoping you'd just let that conversation pass.

HUSBAND What do you want from me? You're driving me crazy.

ANNE I don't know. Sometimes . . . What I want . . .

HUSBAND You want to go away . . . to separate for a while?

ANNE No . . . I don't want that.

HUSBAND *I can't take too much more of this.*

ANNE I don't know what comes over me. Sometimes I want control, physical power, to beat you at some game of strength.

HUSBAND You and what fucking army.

ANNE See? I try to talk to you and you give me this.

HUSBAND What infuriates me is that you keep changing the games on me.

ANNE I do not. I never change the games, do not.

HUSBAND I like this new one. You come home late, I'm tired, and we discuss the latest concepts of monogamy!

ANNE God, you're a jerk. Come on. Come at me. I'm going to wrestle you to the ground and show you something, smart guy.

HUSBAND Oh right . . . spare me! You want to wrestle?

(Anne lunges at him.)

ANNE Focus gives you physical power. *(She twists his arm and gets him in a head lock and somehow forces him to the floor, mostly because she has surprised him.)*

HUSBAND *(He's laughing and enjoying the insanity of it and begins to take control and grabs her.)* What is it about men you don't like?

ANNE Oh, owwww . . . you hurt me . . . Oh God . . . let go . . . please . . .

HUSBAND I'm sorry. You all right?

ANNE Okay . . . I . . . slept with those two guys.

HUSBAND *(He lets go of her . . . He's stunned.)* That's it. I'm out of here. *(As he starts to get up, she pushes him off balance and pins him.)*

ANNE Just kidding. I didn't, I didn't. *(She jumps up.)* I won.

HUSBAND Oh good God. You're killing me. That is not physical prowess . . . get it. You did not beat me and you will never beat me unless you consider a sex change and sports camp . . . goddamn it.

ANNE I feel like I won and that is what counts.

HUSBAND Are you trying to torture me for my past sins? I give up . . . What?

ANNE Now that I beat you, you want to know something else I want? I'll tell you.

HUSBAND I can't wait.

ANNE Look at me and treat me like I'm the most attractive woman you've seen in years. Go ahead, I dare you.

HUSBAND I am capable of that. I can do that. *(Pause.)* Can I walk out of the room and come back in again?

ANNE Yes, you may. *(He exits and comes back in with a different attitude and cooler-looking, maybe with a leather jacket from the closet.)*

HUSBAND I shouldn't have come to your house. I apologize. I don't know what I was thinking.

ANNE I . . . like your jacket.

HUSBAND We've got to talk . . . I just can't be around you without wanting more.

ANNE My husband will kill me.

HUSBAND *(He smiles.)* I know, and he's right . . . He'd probably kill me, too.

ANNE I doubt it.

HUSBAND You are probably right. He's a gentle, sensitive man.

ANNE I don't want to talk about him. What are we going to do?

HUSBAND Nothing . . . Absolutely nothing . . . I'm going to kiss you once goodbye and forever dream. Come here. *(They kiss. It's nice. They stop. He is puzzled. She is delighted and laughs.)* Like it's a joke . . . as if all this is normal conversation. What are you up to? Who do you think I am? I missed one birthday—for God's sake. In fourteen years we've slept apart maybe six months . . .

counting jobs out of town . . . held each other every night . . .
never had problems making love . . . made babies *(Snaps his fin-gers.)* like that . . . kids we like, no less. Doesn't that count?

What we used to be in the sixties . . . Do you think these
things are really games we can play? All the sex we had before
we got together made it possible to grow up. You want to fuck
around again? You can't go back, you know that. That's the sac-rifice, that's one of the vows. How little . . . how nothing! No
more fooling around and we could have all this.

You can't think I don't care what happens. As if we aren't two
sides of the same thing? You can experience wanting someone
else. You are not your mother. I see you. I've got you . . . If you
fall down I'll catch you. But don't make light of it. Don't act
like it's less . . . like this vow doesn't have a life of its own now.
(Pause.)

ANNE I am more than the other half of this vow. Who am I, then?

HUSBAND I know who you are.

ANNE It's not about you or sex. I've lost something and I don't
know what to put in its place. *(Pause.)* You want dinner?

HUSBAND Well, I don't want sweet potatoes. They remind me of
my father.

ANNE Okay, how about couscous?

(HUSBAND exits. ANNE moves stage center.)

SCENE EIGHT

ANNE *in the center talking to the audience as if they were her class.*

ANNE Well, the semester is finally over. It's been quite a struggle,
but we did it. We accomplished the Computer Poetry Project. I

know . . . Dr. Sorenson's class developed a real taste for poetry. Uh-huh . . . Yes, I agree. *(She laughs with them.)* Oh, come on . . . He's hot . . . let's face it . . . I agree. I apologize for my brutal attack on your first papers, but it must have had an effect, because these final papers are outstanding. I actually learned a lot from your observations. I am pleased with everybody's work. Any questions or reflections on what we've done? *(She is surprised at the question and takes a second to answer.)* No, that's fine. I'm fifty. There's a stark reality. *(Students respond.)* If you really look at me, you can see. Focus on my face and you can see my scripts. You call them lines . . . inartistic people call them wrinkles. I will decipher them for you. Between the brows—labor pains. Twice. The little feet around the eyes—those hearty laughs when you were high on whatever. The half moons at the side of the mouth are from years of Christian charity . . . I've smiled sweetly at thousands of truly obnoxious statements. I believe they are poetic. *(Pause.)*

My passions . . . well . . . this has been a semester of passions. Words are one of my passions. Did you know the word "adultery" has more fire than the action. I found that out. I considered it and decided my husband is just my true, instinctive partner. That's very poetic, don't you think?

Close your mouths. A little honesty goes a long way. I am in the middle of my life. I can talk this way because everyone in this room has declared their major in my discipline—Modern American Poetry.

The Golf Ball

›FRANK D. GILROY

'99

ORIGINAL PRODUCTION

DIRECTOR Chris Smith
ASSISTANT DIRECTOR David Winitsky
SET DESIGNER Kenichi Toki
COSTUME DESIGNER Amela Baksic
SOUND Beatrice Terry
PROPS Erika Malone
PRODUCTION STAGE MANAGER Gretchen A. Knowlton
STAGE MANAGER Jim Ring

The cast was as follows:
CHARLIE Baxter Harris
AGNES Mimi Bensinger
GEORGE Tom Ligon

CHARACTERS

CHARLIE George's golf buddy
AGNES POWELL late fifties–early sixties
GEORGE POWELL late fifties–early sixties

PLACE

A wealthy retirement community

TIME

The present

SCENE ONE

GEORGE *and* AGNES POWELL, *at breakfast. She in housecoat, reading a newspaper. He dressed for golf—his clubs visible.*

AGNES *(Head buried in the paper.)* What time do you tee off?

GEORGE Same as always.

AGNES Charlie's late.

GEORGE Hopefully he's overslept, had a flat, won't come at all.

AGNES Here's one for you: A wealthy retired CEO held up a gas station—(GEORGE *snatches the paper from her.)* Pardon *me.*

GEORGE *(Finds the story.)* "Captured by police after a high-speed chase, Mr. A. E. Gantley, former head of Hawking Industries, said, 'It's the most fun I've had in years.' "

AGNES Sounds drunk or senile.

GEORGE *(Reading)* "Mr. Gantley passed a sobriety test and has no history of mental illness."

AGNES Why did he do it, then?

GEORGE Maybe he couldn't face another round of golf.

AGNES Here we go again.

GEORGE *(Reading)* "What the gas station attendant took for a gun proved to be Mr. Gantley's eyeglass case."

AGNES He's lucky he wasn't killed.

GEORGE Or unlucky, depending on his objective.

AGNES Not funny.

GEORGE Not meant to be.

AGNES We're healthy. Our children and grandchildren are fine. We have friends, money. What more do you want?

GEORGE Mrs. Gantley's exact words to Mr. Gantley as he pulled into the gas station intending to say "Fill it up" and said "Stick 'em up" instead.

(AGNES grabs the paper—scans.)

AGNES Where does it say that?

GEORGE I was kidding.

(A car horn sounds.)

AGNES Charlie's here.

GEORGE Alas.

AGNES If you're tired of golf, play tennis; take a bike ride, go swimming.

GEORGE You left out shuffleboard and nature walk.

AGNES Better yet write a book on the dangers of early retirement.

GEORGE Low blow.

AGNES Apologies. For what it's worth, I love you.

GEORGE I love you, too.

(The car horn sounds again impatiently. He kisses her on the cheek; gets his golf clubs.)

AGNES Promise you won't rob a gas station?

GEORGE You have my word. *(He exits.)*

SCENE TWO

A moving car, CHARLIE OLSEN *driving,* GEORGE *beside him.*

CHARLIE I think I found the secret. *(GEORGE remains silent.)* Don't you want to know what it is?

GEORGE More than life.

CHARLIE Concentrate on one thing at a time. Today it's going to be "Take the club back slowly." S-L-O-W-L-Y. Everything else: hip turn, weight distribution, grip, follow-through—I'm putting out of my mind.

GEORGE You're driving too fast.

CHARLIE We're late. We lose our tee-off time, we might not get another.

GEORGE We should be so lucky.

CHARLIE Lucky?

GEORGE If we can't play golf we'll do something else.

CHARLIE My knee rules out tennis, and it's too late to go fishing.

GEORGE I was thinking of something different.

CHARLIE Such as?

GEORGE There's a bank up ahead. What do you say we slip the teller a note saying "Give me all your cash"?

CHARLIE I'd rather play golf.

GEORGE Robbing a gas station would be easier, but I promised Agnes I wouldn't.

CHARLIE *(He's got it now.)* The guy in the paper this morning— Gantley.

GEORGE Right.

CHARLIE He's got to be nuts.

GEORGE I'm not sure.

CHARLIE *(Turning to him.)* A retired CEO robbing a gas station isn't crazy?

GEORGE Keep your eyes on the road.

SCENE THREE

The first tee. CHARLIE *practice-swinging,* GEORGE *standing by.*

CHARLIE *(Bringing the club back in slow motion.)* S-L-O-W-L-Y. Usual stakes?

GEORGE No. Let's make it interesting.

CHARLIE How much?

GEORGE Everything I own against everything you own.

CHARLIE How about twenty a side plus lunch?

GEORGE I said "interesting."

CHARLIE You name it.

GEORGE I did.

CHARLIE *(Going with what he assumes to be a gag)* All I have against all you have?

GEORGE Right.

CHARLIE Including Swiss bank accounts?

GEORGE Everything. What do you say?

CHARLIE It's not fair.

GEORGE Why?

CHARLIE I think I have more than you.

GEORGE I'm worth seven million. What about you?

CHARLIE *(A hint of uneasiness)* What about me?

GEORGE How much money do you have?

CHARLIE *(Trying to make light of it)* I refuse to answer on the grounds—

GEORGE You told me about your mistress—your prostate problems. You won't tell me how much money you have.

CHARLIE What's the punch line?

GEORGE Punch line implies joke. I'm serious.

CHARLIE *(Looking off.)* The starter's waving. We better get going.

(GEORGE reaches into his bag for a ball.)

GEORGE *Damn.*

CHARLIE What is it?

GEORGE I was chipping balls on my lawn—forgot to pack them.

CHARLIE No balls?

GEORGE *(Holding up a ball.)* Except this one.

CHARLIE You better go and get some.

GEORGE You don't think I can play eighteen holes with one ball?

CHARLIE I know so, and I only have a few myself.

GEORGE How much you want to bet?

CHARLIE You've never played eighteen holes without losing two or three balls at least.

GEORGE How much?

CHARLIE I'd be stealing your money.

GEORGE Put up or shut up.

CHARLIE *(Irritated)* *Five hundred bucks.*

GEORGE You're on. *(Regarding the ball)* It's a Titleist One. *(Hands the ball to Charlie.)* Write your initials on it.

CHARLIE I trust you.

GEORGE I insist.

CHARLIE You're not serious about this?

GEORGE Trying to weasel out of it?

(CHARLIE initials the ball, hands it to GEORGE.)

CHARLIE Your honor.

(GEORGE tees up; prepares to hit.)

SCENE FOUR

In the rough. GEORGE *looking for his ball.* CHARLIE *standing by.*

CHARLIE How much longer?

GEORGE Till I find it.

CHARLIE There's a foursome breathing down our necks.

GEORGE Wave them through.

CHARLIE At this rate we'll be all day.

GEORGE You're in a hurry, go. I'll catch up.

CHARLIE You've been looking for fifteen minutes.

GEORGE Is there a time limit?

CHARLIE The bet's off. I'll give you another ball.

GEORGE *The bet's on.*

CHARLIE *(Glancing back.)* That foursome's teeing off. I'm going, George.

GEORGE See you later.

CHARLIE I'm stopping for lunch after nine holes.

GEORGE Save me a seat.

(CHARLIE *goes off.* GEORGE *resumes the search.*)

SCENE FIVE

The clubhouse. CHARLIE *at lunch.* GEORGE *appears.*

CHARLIE Look who's here . . . Well?

GEORGE Guess.

CHARLIE You couldn't find it.

GEORGE Guess again.

CHARLIE You found it, but then you lost it again.

GEORGE Right.

CHARLIE Make the check out to cash.

GEORGE I lost it and found it three times. *(Displaying the ball.)* Note the letters "C.H." in your own inimitable hand.

CHARLIE *(Inspecting the ball.)* You played all nine holes?

GEORGE Shot a fifty-three—my best score ever.

CHARLIE You've still got nine to go, and the back side's a lot tougher.

GEORGE Care to make it a thousand?

CHARLIE What about the sixteenth hole?

GEORGE What about it?

CHARLIE You usually drop your ball on the other side of the pond and take a penalty.

GEORGE No drop today.

CHARLIE You're going to try and hit across?

GEORGE I *am* going to hit across.

CHARLIE You've never cleared the water in all the times we played.

GEORGE A thousand too rich for your blood?

CHARLIE *A thousand it is.*

SCENE SIX

The sixteenth tee. GEORGE *and* CHARLIE *arrive.*

GEORGE *(Displaying the ball.)* Fifteen down and three holes to go. Getting nervous?

CHARLIE Don't look now, but that water staring you in the face is two hundred yards across.

GEORGE *(To the ball)* Is he trying to rattle us?

CHARLIE Use the ladies' tee. Give yourself a chance at least.

GEORGE No thanks. My honor?

CHARLIE Right.

GEORGE Last chance to increase your wager.

CHARLIE I feel guilty enough as it is.

GEORGE *(To the ball)* Till we meet again.

CHARLIE What you mean is goodbye forever. *(GEORGE tees up, takes several practice swings. Pauses . . . focuses . . . concentrates . . . hits. Impressed) Wow.*

(Both men follow the ball's flight.)

GEORGE What do you think?

CHARLIE Best drive you ever hit.

GEORGE It's got a chance.

CHARLIE It's going to be close.

GEORGE *Get up there—get up there!*

(Both men follow the ball's trajectory to a watery finish.) Splash.

CHARLIE No cigar, but one helluva try.

GEORGE Five yards short?

CHARLIE Give or take.

GEORGE *(Marking where the ball landed.)* On a line with that willow tree and the flag stick?

CHARLIE What difference does it make?

GEORGE Lucky it's summer.

CHARLIE Why?

GEORGE The water will be warm.

CHARLIE You're not thinking—

GEORGE —If the fat lady sang, I missed it.

SCENE SEVEN

Beside the pond. GEORGE *removing shoes, socks, and rolling up his pants.*
CHARLIE *incredulous.*

CHARLIE There are snakes in there. Snapping turtles. God knows
what.

GEORGE I haven't done this since I was a kid.

CHARLIE What are people going to think?

GEORGE Frankly, I don't give a damn.

CHARLIE You're beginning to worry me.

GEORGE *(Pants rolled—sighting.)* Flag stick—willow—tee. Line
them up like so and the ball should be right about there. *(Pointing.)* What do you think?

CHARLIE I'm leaving, George.

GEORGE Would you mind calling Agnes and telling her I'll be late?

SCENE EIGHT

The Powells' kitchen. AGNES *lost in thought.* GEORGE, *bearing his golf
clubs, enters.*

AGNES At last.

GEORGE Didn't Charlie tell you I'd be late?

AGNES Yes.

(The phone beside her rings. She ignores it.)

GEORGE Aren't you going to answer it?

AGNES It'll be someone asking if you're all right. I've had a dozen
calls like that so far.

GEORGE I'm fine. Why wouldn't I be?

AGNES A prominent citizen with his pants rolled trying to find a golf ball in a filthy pond makes people wonder.

GEORGE What did you tell them?

AGNES Observe. *(She picks up the ringing phone.)* Hello? . . . Hi, Madge . . . Correct . . . Pants rolled—wading . . . Because Charlie bet him he couldn't play eighteen holes without losing a ball . . . I hope you're right . . . Bye. *(She hangs up.)*

GEORGE You hope she's right about what?

AGNES She said, "Boys will be boys."

GEORGE A dozen calls?

AGNES At least. You frightened Charlie.

GEORGE He scares easy.

AGNES You frightened *me* and I don't scare easy.

GEORGE What's for supper—I'm famished.

AGNES Charlie said you should give it to the Red Cross.

GEORGE It?

AGNES The thousand dollars.

GEORGE He hasn't won yet.

AGNES Does that mean you're going to keep looking for the ball?

GEORGE I don't have to look for it. *(Revealing the ball.)* Voilà!

AGNES You found it?

GEORGE Just as the sun set.

AGNES It's over, then.

GEORGE Almost.

AGNES Almost?

GEORGE I've got two holes to go.

AGNES I'm sure Charlie will concede.

GEORGE That's not the point.

AGNES What *is* the point, George?

GEORGE I have to play the last two holes.

AGNES Hook your tee shot on the eighteenth, you're back in the pond again.

GEORGE I'll slice deliberately.

AGNES Suppose the ball hits a sprinkler or the cart path and bounces into the water?

GEORGE The odds against that are incalculable.

AGNES One of the calls was from the club president quoting the rule that forbids members from entering water hazards.

GEORGE This ball will not end up in the water.

AGNES But if by some miracle it does, will you admit defeat?

GEORGE I can't.

AGNES You'll roll up your pants and wade in?

GEORGE Yes.

AGNES For how long?

GEORGE Until I find it.

AGNES We'll be kicked out of the club, ridiculed, lose our friends.

GEORGE Would that be the end of the world?

AGNES It would be the end of *my* world. Not the world I fancied as a child but the world I'm stuck with and intend to make the best of.

GEORGE Stuck with?

AGNES *Stuck with.* Don't you think *Mrs.* Gantley ever felt like robbing a gas station?

GEORGE It's different for men.

AGNES Right. *You* pick the dream. *We* tag along. If it doesn't end up the way we hoped, we grin and bear it.

GEORGE You knew what my goals were before we married.

AGNES True.

GEORGE You encouraged and supported them.

AGNES Also true.

GEORGE Did I accomplish everything I said I would?

AGNES Yes. And there's the rub.

GEORGE What do you mean?

AGNES You dreamed too small.

GEORGE You never complained before.

AGNES You never waded in a scummy pond looking for a golf ball before.

GEORGE You win: I won't play the last two holes.

AGNES I'm afraid you have to.

GEORGE Why?

AGNES If you don't we'd always wonder what difference it might have made.

GEORGE Suppose by some fluke the ball goes in the water?

AGNES And you look for it?

GEORGE Yes.

AGNES When you come home I'll be gone.

GEORGE Why?

AGNES I don't believe in flukes.

GEORGE Where will you go?

AGNES First to visit Mrs. Gantley. After that who knows.

GEORGE I'm going out early in the morning. Two holes—I'll be back in time for breakfast.

AGNES I hope so, George. *(Touching his cheek lovingly.)* I really do.

GEORGE It'll be a breeze thanks to a tip from Charlie. He said forget about everything except taking the club back slowly. *(He takes a driver from his bag. Sets the golf ball on the floor. His back to her, he demonstrates.)* S-L-O-W-L-Y. *(As he spells and takes the club back,* AGNES *exits.)* What do you think? *(When she doesn't respond, he turns—finds her gone.)* Agnes? . . . Agnes? . . .

(Lights narrow on the golf ball.)

Dreamtime for Alice

'99

›SUSAN KIM

ORIGINAL PRODUCTION

DIRECTOR Richard Lichte
SET DESIGNER Kenichi Toki
COSTUME DESIGNER Amela Baksic
SOUND Beatrice Terry
PROPS Erika Malone
PRODUCTION STAGE MANAGER Gretchen A. Knowlton
STAGE MANAGER Page Van Denburg

The cast was as follows:
ALICE Cecilia deWolf
ANNOUNCER Julie McKee

CHARACTERS

ANNOUNCER bright, upbeat, female, Australian. The voice of professional tour guides and stewardesses everywhere

ALICE an upper-middle-class, educated white or Asian woman in her mid-forties. She is brittle, assured, and glib on the surface, and full of rage, fear, and mollusk vulnerability underneath. She is hatless, in shorts, sandals, T-shirt, and blouse. She carries a painted cloth "dilly" bag

PLACE

A modest tourist stop in central Australia, in the outback, about seventy miles north of Alice Springs. It consists basically of a very minor kind of rock outcropping, a bit of which is visible upstage left.

NOTE

There are unspecific shifts in time as the day lengthens and ends, to be indicated by lighting and sound cues.

In darkness, the sound of a lone didgeridoo. It cuts out abruptly. The voice of a cheerful Australian female.

ANNOUNCER Attention, ladies and gentlemen, boys and girls. Cheryl here again, and we hope you're enjoying your Outback Adventure Tour. We're about a hundred and twenty kilometers outside Alice Springs, winding around the MacDonnell Range on our way to Ayers Rock. Your photo opportunity is just about up, so please get back on board the bus; we'll be continuing westward seventy-five kilometers to our next point of interest, Corroboree Rock, where you can buy souvenirs, have a cuppa tea, and, most important, have that wee you've probably been worrying about. And remember: Australia has the highest skin cancer rates in the world, so keep your heads covered.

(The sound of a bus roaring away. Lights up. A modest tourist stop in the Australian outback. It is very bright, very hot. A minute overhang of rock is upstage. ALICE *stands reading from an Australian guidebook, a camera around her neck.)*

ALICE "Dreaming. To aborigines, the state of knowledge that relates all objects and beings to one another by a complex series of myths. The dreamtime was the time of creation, when the world was forged by powerful beings who still walk the outback, controlling universal destiny." *(She glances around, and checks her guidebook again.)* According to the dreaming, every rock, every tree, every creature has a place in the cosmic order and a reason for being. That boulder. The clouds. Every living thing. We are all accounted for. We all have a place in the dreaming. *(Slaps at an insect on her neck.)* The reason I'm here in the Australian outback is because I am forty-three years old and I've never had an adventure. Not once. Not unless you include fourteen years of marriage to a psychopath. *(She lifts her camera and gazes through it around her, as if through binoculars.)* I don't have much to say about Stan except that I have the distinct feeling he's *not* accounted for in the dreaming. When he wasn't telling loud, unfunny jokes or getting into screaming fights with strangers, he'd be tossing down gimlets and margaritas and stingers and punching things around me. Never me directly, but always something *next* to me. Walls, mirrors, the refrigerator. The air. For years I actually thought this meant there wasn't a problem.

Anyway, that's enough about Stan. I'm here because he's not. I'm here to enjoy myself and forget all about him. *(Beat.)* All right. What happened was, last Tuesday, Stan and I had "words," as the saying goes, and it came out that Stan has, *quelle surprise*, a girlfriend. He's been seeing her for over a year, someone I actually know, our accountant Sorrel—yes, I'm afraid we have an accountant named Sorrel—and he informed me that not only were they madly in love, but the two of them were flying to Impruneta for three weeks. In Tuscany. In Italy.

So what do you do at moments like that? Well, what are your options? Do you (A) fly into an unattractive rage? (B) wait it out, since it's only sex, and how long can that last, anyway? Or do you simply (C) walk away from fourteen years, a life, a home, the whole ball of wax?

I don't know. I honestly don't.

All I knew was that I needed distance, space, and anonymity. So forty-eight hours later, give or take, I too was winging my way to a foreign country. To Alice Springs, Australia. Seeing as my name is Alice, it seemed only . . .

(She notices something.)

Oh my God.

(She shades her eyes.)

Oh my God, it's a *dingo*. Mrs. Schwartzbaum? It's a real live dingo. Come quick before it gets away!

And bring your camera! It's in that clump of bushes, it's yellow, and . . . oh my God, it's got something in his mouth. It's got a *baby* in its mouth! Just kidding, Mrs. Schwartzbaum. Mrs. Schwartzbaum?

(She looks offstage.)

That's funny . . . she was right behind me . . .

(She walks offstage.)

Hello? Anybody? HELLLLO!

(Beat. She walks back on.)

Huh.

(She crosses off in the other direction. Pause. She crosses back on.)

Don't you just hate this kind of crap?

(She looks at her watch.)

I hate to say it. I really hate to say it, but do you know what's going through my mind? I think she did it on purpose. That bitch Cheryl. Why I don't know, but you don't just *leave* someone in the outback. You don't just leave an American *citizen* in the middle of the freaking *desert*. Vicious, passive/aggressive Australian *cow* . . .

(She shades her eyes, looking off.)

Sorry. Hostility alert. My therapist says I have "hostility issues." Meaning I spent so many years *not* expressing anger that it's finally gotten to the point where I honestly feel I don't have any, which even *I* know can't be true. Only lately it's been starting to build up and occasionally spurt out in totally inappropriate ways and at the oddest people. Isn't it funny how you don't even have to have kids to turn into your own mother?

I don't think everyone is out to get me, by the way. I actually made a friend on the bus. Mrs. Schwartzbaum? She's this very charming, incredibly dapper little woman from Berlin. You'd think she might be wondering where I was, unless of course we hadn't hit it off as much as I thought. Which seems to be a recurrent theme in my life, as I've recently discovered.

(Beat. She takes out a compact and powders her nose.)

One may be wondering if I'm starting to panic. I'm not. I'm an American tourist, you don't just lose an American tourist like that. At least not with the dollar the way it is these days. Besides, I'm all set. See?

(She rummages through her bag and takes out a small bottle of spring water, a PowerBar, and a Swiss army knife.)

Look—this one not only has the saw attachment but the little corkscrew as well. If I run into any aborigine sommeliers, I'm all set. Once a Wellesley girl, always a Wellesley girl.

(Puts them away.)

Anyway, I expect Cheryl will be realizing her mistake any second now. I expect that big gray bus will come roaring back down the road, and let me tell you one thing, I'm writing one very nasty letter to Outback Adventure Tours as soon as I get back to my room.

(Notices something off.)

Oh Christ. All right, that's enough. Shoo! Go on!

(Stamps her foot.)

Some of the local fauna are mildly interesting, but only at a distance. An *extreme* distance, I might add.

(To animal)

That especially goes for lizards. I bet you're incredibly poisonous, aren't you? Nasty thing.

(Claps her hands.)

Now beat it! Go on!

(She notices her arm and examines it for sunburn.)

Oh crap. Now what?

(She pokes it. She glances around and notices the tiny outcropping of rock. She stands under it. It provides virtually no cover whatsoever.)

I just worry about this sun. It really is true that you can't appreciate how intense it is because it's so dry out here, and God knows the last thing I want is any more wrinkles. Some people are very proud about getting older, they say they don't mind all those little dings and dents and scars you accumulate over the

years, but my feeling is, they're lying. As for me, I'm holding on
as long as I . . .

(Notices something off. In a whisper)

Oh my good God Jesus Christ, would you look at that.

Parrots. *Hundreds* of them. Turquoise-blue like the Caribbean
Sea, speaking of my least favorite island chain in the world.

(In her regular voice)

All right . . . that's enough. Move along now. Go on!

(Claps her hands. They take off.)

It's like some kind of *freak* show around here.

Anyway—about the sun? Epidermally speaking, this kind of
sun is a killer. Have you ever been to New Mexico and just
taken a look at the people who live there? They're like handbags
with legs. I'm not making this up. My uncle lived in Albu-
querque, and by the time he was sixty he had melanomas the
size of silver dollars all over his entire body. He looked like a
package of Wonder Bread. And of course I didn't bring a hat,
because I didn't think I'd be getting out of the goddamn bus.

(Cocks her head.)

Is that them? No? Christ, what am I, invisible? Do I make so
little impression? How is it possible that not a single person on
that entire bus notices I'm not around anymore?

Jesus.

(Takes out a bottle of sunscreen and applies it to her face and arms.)

You see, I'm secretly very vain about my skin. That sounds
silly, doesn't it? I mean, skin, big deal, what's to be proud of,
right? It's not like having a beautiful face or endless legs or a
massive set of knockers. None of which I have, as you may have
already noticed. And if you haven't, just ask my husband. But
for years—and this is the God's truth—my skin has been as soft

as it was when I was a little girl. And when Stan and I first started dating, he used to touch me so gently, just with the tips of his fingers, as if he couldn't believe that underneath all the clothes and words and *things* on top, I could be so . . . Well, trust me. It's always been my best feature.

(She finishes and puts it away. Indicates her painted cloth bag.)

I just bought this at the airport gift shop in Sydney. It's called a "dilly" bag. If Stan were here, he'd probably say something like "It's a real dilly, all right, Alice. You really know how to pick 'em."

I wish I had my hat with me.

(She takes her outer blouse and ties it on her head. It is very hot. Lights shift.)

(Lights up, ALICE *sits reading her book and eating her PowerBar.)*

ALICE Well, that's very interesting.

This is the story about the creation of Uluru . . . "Uluru" being the aboriginal name for Ayers Rock, for anyone who gives a rat's ass. According to myth, Uluru was initially created by two little boys at play, and then it was subsequently molded by all the desert animals who lived nearby. Like the poisonous snake and the devil dingo.

"The devil dingo."

Now I don't know about anyone else, but I find that oddly charming.

(She fans herself with the book, licking her lips.)

Jesus, my throat. I feel like I've swallowed a Fair Isle sweater. I think it's time for a little visit to the bar, don't you?

(Takes out her water.)

Don't worry . . . I'm only allowing myself a sip at a time. I shall drink sparingly, as of the blood of Christ.

(She takes a sip. It is rather longer than it should be. As she drinks, she notices something on the rock next to her. She screams, spilling some water as she jumps up. Claps her hands.)

All right. Beat it! C'mon . . . get lost!

(She takes off a sandal and considers smashing whatever it is . . . but it escapes.)

Goddamn spiders.

(She recaps the bottle and puts it away.)

One may be wondering why I chose Australia in the first place. I'm clearly not too keen on wildlife, or heat, or an entire nation of people descended from felons, come to think of it, so why Australia? Why not someplace *normal*, like . . . Europe? Excluding Tuscany, of course. Well, I'll tell you why not Europe, there are too many goddamn churches. I'm serious.

Well then, why the outback? Why this unintentional walkabout? Not that I'm actually *walking* here, and not that I know what a walkabout is exactly. A person . . . walking about, I suppose. But that's what I like about all this, you see. How mysterious it is. How *weird*. Sere and lifeless like it's been scorched by a meteor. Because this . . .

(Indicates horizon.)

. . . all this is exactly how I look on the inside. Minus the parrots. See, for all its weirdness and otherness . . . I feel like I *know* this place in some funny way, I fit in somehow, like I was here in a previous life. Or if I don't fit in, I could somehow. If only I could figure out how. And what would that bring me? Some kind of epiphany, I suppose? Some kind of answer?

Well, all right, then. The real reason is, I haven't done much traveling in my life, certainly not by myself, and it frankly makes me a little nervous. The only place a certain person would go to was the Caribbean. And don't ask which island, they're all essentially the same, and besides which, it doesn't matter, we went to all of them. Which makes the Tuscan villa a little hard to digest.

Anyway . . . the bottom line is, I wanted to go as literally and physically as far as I could from Englewood Cliffs—to the *antipodes* of New Jersey—and still be able to speak English. I know . . . small of me, isn't it? Because the English language is my crutch. That much I'm not ashamed to admit. I'm an editor at a mid-sized publishing house, and a voracious reader and occasional writer, and words are what I do for a living. They're what I consider . . .

(She notices something.)

Oh, thank Christ, it's about frigging time.

Jesus God in heaven, thank you, thank you, Mother Mary, Mama's goin' home . . .

(She jumps up and runs downstage, waving.)

Hello! Over here! Hellooo!

(She slowly stops. She squints, rubbing her eyes. She laughs.)

Well, talk about dubious accomplishments—I've had my first hallucination. But, Jesus Christ, I could have sworn . . .

I'm not religious, by the way. I know I mention God and Christ an awful lot, it may even look like I'm trying to petition them, but believe me, I'm not. The words just blip out of me sometimes, like . . . religious Tourette's. Of course if your parents dragged you to church every Sunday for eighteen years, you'd know what I was talking about. It imprints on your brain in a very sinister way. Part of it always stays with you, like a vestigial . . . flipper.

(She goes back to the rock, opens her knife.)

Actually, that's not completely true, is it?

(She begins to carve in the rock.)

I can honestly say I don't believe in God, and never did . . .
but wasn't there a time I was willing to give him a chance?
What was I, eleven? twelve? I had this friend Mary. Mary
Chaney. She went to Quaker meeting every Sunday with her
family, and one day she asked if I wanted to go with them. So I
did, and the only thing I remember was that this really old guy,
although of course in retrospect he was probably like *thirty*,
stood up and said, "We are not here to speak to God. We are
here for God to speak to us." Aha, I thought. So I sat there, very
patiently, and waited for God to speak to me. I waited and
waited and waited, and guess what, He didn't. Or if He did, He
certainly didn't introduce Himself. So needless to say, after an
hour had gone by, I stopped waiting for Him. And eventually I
stopped waiting altogether.

(She stands back to admire her work a moment: the word Alice. *Then she
continues carving.)*

I know it looks like I'm defacing an aboriginal shrine here,
but to be honest, I really don't give a shit. Besides, I think I've
earned the right to let people know I was here. How else will
my children be able to pinpoint where the scrappy old matriarch
was lost before she was finally rescued?

I'm being figurative, by the way, I don't actually *have* any
children. Stan again, of course. He never said no definitively, it
was always the final bargaining chip, the last manipulative ploy
in any argument we were having. How can we possibly have
kids if you—fill in the blank. Take that job? Don't trust me
with our finances? Hang over my head all the time like a freaking harpy? I don't know, maybe it was for the best. Yeah . . .
like No shit, Sherlock. But it's the single thing in fourteen years
I almost left him over. And I never did. And now, of course, it's
too late, I'm too . . . umm . . .

(She licks her lips.)

Christ, if only I had more water. Maybe I can just wet my whistle. Maybe I can just rinse out my mouth with water and then spit it back in the bottle.

(She undoes the bottle, empties the contents into her mouth, and swishes it around.)

Mmmmmmmmmmm.

(She swallows, wipes her mouth.)

Someone will be here soon. I know someone will be here very soon.

(She empties the final drops into her mouth and continues carving. Lights shift.)

(Lights up. The words "Alice was here" are carved in the rock. ALICE *draws in the dirt with a pebble.)*

Try to remember. How far is it from here back to town? What did she say? Fifty kilometers? A hundred? So how much is that in miles? A ten-K road race is a little over six miles, so a *hundred* K is sixty miles plus. If I wait until the sun sets, how long would it take me to run back to town?

Christ, who am I kidding?

But it's a choice. At least I have some autonomy here. What if I were to travel *half* the distance? I could walk thirty miles, couldn't I?

Well . . . what if I were to divide that in half? And what if I were to divide that in half? And then that in half? Jesus, that's very interesting. When would it ever end?

It wouldn't, would it.

Because mathematically speaking, if you kept dividing a distance in half—over and over, to the minutest subatomic level—there are always an infinite number of points between two places—between here and civilization.

But that's just an intellectual construct. I'm just freaking myself out by breaking it down like that. What's that called again? Something-something-or-other? "How can you travel over an infinite series of points in a finite amount of time?" Zeno's paradox. So what was the answer?

The answer is, you can't.

Screw it all, of course you can. The reality is, you just do it. You just step forward. So step forward. Come on, Alice . . . do something. Spring, Alice. See Alice spring. Spring, Alice, spring.

(She doesn't move. Lights shift.)

(Lights up. ALICE *is sitting against the rock. She is going through the items in her wallet one by one.)*

ALICE Amoco card.

Amex. MasterCard, soon to expire.

Driver's license. God, and people wonder why I hate getting my picture taken.

(She puts everything back in her wallet.)

See, I'm trying very hard not to think about that piece of rock jutting out above my head. About half an hour ago, I noticed something very strange. I noticed it was covered with water, trickling out of that crack at the top. But the thing is, it's not, really. I know it's not. You'd have to be an idiot to believe that any kind of water out here is even a remote possibility, it's so freaking dry I can't even sweat anymore, I can hardly *blink*. It's obviously some kind of illusion. And that's why I haven't bothered getting up to check it—because I refuse to give in to wishful thinking. Because if I do, if I get up and start to desperately suck rock, I will have lost something crucial here. My dignity? No. It's more basic than that. My identity. I am a rational person, I know deep in the core of my animal brain that there are no miracles, there is no divine intervention, and there is no water. And the last thing I can do for myself, the last positive action I can take, is to not give in to false hope based on illusion.

But it's so damned *hard*. It's incredible what this heat can do to one's perceptions. For instance, I never really believed in mirages. I always thought they were something in the movies, like quicksand . . . I mean, real to an extent, but not to the point of seeing palm trees or dancing girls or the Taj Mahal shimmering in the horizon. But they really do exist. Only out here, mirages don't look like water. They look like ice. Isn't that odd? It looks as if I'm surrounded by polar ice caps, fields of snow, sheets of blue crackling ice. And underneath, everything shimmers like ghosts, like it's all a memory of something that happened long ago.

See, if I let myself, I can actually see things from my past.

I'm serious. Look over there . . . I can see the broken sidewalk in front of our house in Providence, and the big oaks on either side. I can see snow falling over the Manhattan skyline the first winter I lived there. And I see blue. Blue, blue water.

What summer was that? My sixth? My seventh? I have on a big life jacket. I can feel the sun on my face, my knees tucked up tight to my chest . . . drifting farther and farther away from shore, until all I can see around me is ocean and water. And faraway voices so tiny, like insects on the horizon . . .

(The faraway buzz of an airplane. She opens her eyes.)

What's that?

(She scans the sky.)

What is it, am I starting to hear things now? Is that real? Is it real or am I making it up? Oh God. Oh Jesus, it's real, it's real . . .

(She fumbles through her dilly bag, emptying it onto the ground and scrabbling through the contents as the noise gets louder.)

Christ, don't I have a mirror in here? A compact? Anything? Eye pencil, lip pencil . . . shit! Help! I'm down here! Goddamn you, help me, I'm down here!

(She jumps up, pulling off her turban and waving it like a flag.)

Jesus Christ, why don't you see me? I'm right down here! Open your goddamn eyes and notice me!

(She stops waving her shirt.)

Fire. I've got to build a fire. Idiot, why didn't I think of that before?

(She crosses off and runs back on.)

Shit! And there's no wood because there aren't any goddamn trees!

(She crosses off and returns with some dead brush. She throws it down.)

If they come back, they'll be able to see it. They should be able to see for miles . . .

(She scrabbles through her bag, emptying it on the ground. Fishes out a pack of cigarettes and hurls them down.)

No. No. Please, dear God, don't tell me that today of all days I don't have any *matches.*

(She slams down her bag in frustration. She stares at the trash by her feet; then she bends down and picks up a pair of reading glasses.)

Jesus Christ, I am not going to die.

(She goes to the woodpile and tries to use one of the lenses to magnify sunlight.)

This has to work. There's so much sunlight, it just has to work. Come on. Come on, you can do it.

(She continues trying to make a fire. The buzzing grows fainter and finally dies away completely. ALICE *continues working feverishly. She finally slams down her glasses in frustration and bursts into tears.)*

Fire fire everywhere, not a flame to drink.

(She wipes her face. She tastes her tears. She starts to ravenously wipe her face with her hands and licks them as she continues to weep silently. Lights shift.)

(Lights up. It is dusk. The woodpile is untouched. ALICE *is huddled against the rock, her shirt wrapped around her.)*

ALICE Hey. I can see you. Don't be so damn coy. Yes, you. Behind the rock. You could at least come out so we can communicate properly. One on one.

Do you mind my asking a personal question? Why do they call you the "devil dingo"? Out of all the indigenous fauna, I'm sure there are others more devilish-looking than you. You're actually a fairly attractive species, as predators go.

Recognizable, at least. You might say, almost familiar. You remind me a little of old Spangle. She was half spaniel, half beagle, hence Spangle. Get it?

Jesus, I haven't thought of her in years.

So can I ask you bluntly? *Are* you actually the devil?

Because I don't believe in you, if you are. Nothing personal. For one thing, I know this is all a dream. I'm dreaming here. I just wanted to make that clear before this goes any further.

Was that you making all that racket a few minutes ago? Actually, there seems to be more than one of you, unless this hallucination is going further than I thought. A lot more of you would be my guess. I'm not sure where you all are exactly, but you seem to be getting closer.

Hey, I have a swell idea. I have part of a PowerBar that I'd love to share with you and your compadres. It's peanut butter–mocha, which you'll have to take my word for is better than it sounds. Would you like the rest of it?

(She holds it out with difficulty.)

I can't throw it. If you want it, you're going to have to come and get it. No?

I almost wish you *were* the devil. That way you could at least answer a few questions that have been bothering me. Like if this is hell, why am I so goddamn cold? It feels like the temperature's dropped eighty degrees in the past hour. I'm freezing to death.

Are the ice caps closing in?

I wish you could take me around a little. Show me the sights. After all, this is all yours, isn't it? The landscape, I mean. The sky. This rock. According to my book, you made damn near everything around here, didn't you?

Hey, I just thought of something. If "god" is "dog" spelled backwards, then "dingo" spelled backwards is . . . "ognid."

(She laughs. The sound of dingoes yapping.)

Jesus.

Hey, was that you who made the water appear? You know. Out of the rock up there. That was a pretty neat trick, I must say. You'll have to explain how you did that to me sometime. I bet it was you who turned the temperature down, too, wasn't it?

Can I ask you why?

You don't say. It was to make me feel better?

Well, that's damned thoughtful of you. I suppose I should thank you. Unfortunately, that reminds me of something I read somewhere. When a predator kills something, when a lion sinks its teeth into the neck of a gazelle, say, there's a sudden burst of endorphins in the dying animal. It's a final goodie, a last-second burst of pleasure, a bone nature throws you for being such a good little victim. Is that what you're doing?

Well, if it is, count me out. I don't want any of your pity.

(A dog growls.)

Oh Christ. Please, not yet.

Who are you, anyway? Are you God? Or are you the devil? Not that I honestly give a damn, because I don't. All I want to know is, do you have any pull here? Because I really don't want to die. Not out here, anyway. Not like this.

Look, I'm not going to lie to you. I don't have any illusions about who I am. I'm not a saint, and if truth be told, I'm not even especially nice. I'm middle-aged, middle-class, and middle-of-the-road; and if you really took a hard look at my life, if you were really honest, I guess you could say I've blown it. I wasted it all on a career I stopped caring about years ago and a marriage I should have left but I didn't, and everything else, anything that could have meant something over the years, could have *defined* me, I methodically aborted and squashed down and talked myself out of one by one. I mean, I wanted to be a writer once upon a time. I wanted children, I wanted to fucking *travel*. But I'd always held everything back, everything I ever really wanted or thought or felt, to the point where I can't even remember what they are.

Now why did I do that?

I think I did it because—somewhere along the line—I got the idea that that's what I was *supposed* to be doing. That that's what being *good* was. And that somehow, secretly, you were watching me all along.

But were you? And if you were, did you honestly care? Did you ever care about any of it?

(The dog whimpers. ALICE *gets to her knees.)*

Look.

I'm groveling without irony. I'm actually *praying* for the first time in years, I don't even remember how the words go. I'm praying for my life.

I can't bargain with you. I'm not going to say I'm going to give you anything. For one thing, even with my smart-ass atheism, I really doubt it works that way. And besides, I honestly don't think I have anything you could possibly want. Because I don't have anything left.

(She upends her bag.)

I mean, what. Money? You couldn't possibly want that. My identification, then? My credit? Any skin-care products?

See? There's nothing. Nothing left at all. Just me and my shadow. All my flaws, my sins of omission. All my weaknesses and stubbornness and pride.

(Sound of barking, which subsides to a whimper.)

What?

You don't mean that, do you. You actually want them?

You're kidding, right?

Well. In that case, take my flaws. Please. Straight deal, even-Steven. Just try not to spend them all in one place, okay?

(She leans back against the rock and shuts her eyes. The sound of whimpering dies down and then stops.)

Oh. And amen.

My mother used to come into my room every night to pray. She'd kneel next to me in the dark, and I'd mimic her. I'd put my hands together and bow my head down to the covers, and I'd repeat those mumbling words that seemed so strange. And invariably the sound would wake Spangle from her doggy dreams beneath the bed . . . and she'd creep over to me, and she'd nuzzle my hands with her cold, wet nose, and I'd hear the

thump of her tail on the floor. And I'd kneel there, secretly
stroking her soft muzzle, my mother next to me. And we'd pray.
(Beat. A faint light plays on her face.)

How strange. I can almost hear something. A rumbling
sound from far away. Is it the ice caps again?

Is it a car?

Or is it another illusion?

*(The light grows brighter. ALICE opens her eyes and stares straight out,
waiting. The light grows impossibly bright. Lights slowly fade to black.)*

Goodbye, Oscar

'99

›ROMULUS LINNEY

ORIGINAL PRODUCTION

DIRECTOR Peter Maloney
SET DESIGNER Kris Stone
COSTUME DESIGNER Amela Baksic
SOUND Beatrice Terry
PROPS Erika Malone
PRODUCTION STAGE MANAGER Gretchen A. Knowlton
STAGE MANAGER Paul A. Powell

The cast was as follows:
OSCAR Jack Gilpin
YOUNG GENTLEMAN Dashiell Eaves

CHARACTERS

OSCAR WILDE

A YOUNG GENTLEMAN

PLACE

Hotel D'Alsace, Paris

TIME

November 30, 1900

English band music, but soft and distorted.

    A table and two chairs. A coat tree with several coats, a hat, and a cane. Smaller table to one side, holding a tray, two glasses, and a bottle of absinthe.

    OSCAR WILDE *sits at the table, in shirtsleeves, back to us. A* YOUNG GENTLEMAN *enters. He is dressed in modern casual clothes.*

YOUNG GENTLEMAN He says he is fighting a duel to the death with his wallpaper. He says he is dying beyond his means. His body is bloated and toxic. He is almost dead. Fever rises. Delirium, to wander in mind. He is young again. He thinks he leaves his bed in the Hotel D'Alsace. (*He takes a fur-lined overcoat from the coat tree, hands it to* OSCAR, *who puts it on and walks about.*) He thinks he is wearing his fur-lined coat, watching in trains the great suns and moons of the United States of America. He thinks he arrives in Leadville, Colorado, where in fact he did once lecture Americans on good taste. Again he admires miners, their clothes clean in the morning, in their wide-brimmed hats, bandannas, boots, and cloaks. He calls them the best-dressed men in America. (*The* YOUNG GENTLEMAN *escorts* OSCAR *about.*) He goes again with a lecherous old man to a Leadville brothel. The ladies enjoy his accent and at the New Testament he recites in Greek, they laugh. (OSCAR *stands up, drunk.*) But they listen to his poem about Jesus and the Whore.

OSCAR Your lovers are not dead, I know, they will rise up and hear your voice and clash their cymbals and rejoice, and run to kiss your mouth, have no fear, only one God has ever died, only one God has ever let his side be pierced by the soldier's spear.

(*He almost falls. The* YOUNG GENTLEMAN *escorts* OSCAR *back to his chair.*)

YOUNG GENTLEMAN The old man tried to get Oscar drunk, but Oscar could outdrink cowboys, never mind old men, and will not sleep with him. Very well, says the old man, being a good sport, and he pays me to help Oscar back to his hotel, arranges a treat for him. (*He pulls the table downstage and places the two chairs by it. He helps* OSCAR *off with his coat.*) Don't go to bed yet, the old man said. Just wait.

(*He leaves* OSCAR, *goes to the costume rack, puts on the jacket of a poor bellhop. He becomes a young* BOY *and knocks on an imaginary door.*)

OSCAR Yes? Come in.

(*Enter* BOY. *He has a bottle and two glasses.*)

BOY Good evening!

OSCAR Oh. (*Pause.*) Good evening.

BOY May I join you? (*Pause.*) Oscar, right?

OSCAR Yes. Did an old man send you?

BOY Yes.

OSCAR Did he tell you why?

BOY He asked me to come in his place.

OSCAR What do you think he meant?

BOY Keep you company.

OSCAR Would you enjoy that?

BOY Oh, sure.

OSCAR Are you certain?

BOY Yeah!

OSCAR Well, then. Would you like some of that? What is it?

BOY The old man said you liked absinthe.

OSCAR I do. I'll pour. *(OSCAR pours absinthe for them. The* BOY *takes off his hotel jacket and sits waiting.* OSCAR *hands him an absinthe.)* To your good health.

BOY Yours. *(He drinks, then chokes, coughs.)*

OSCAR Sip. It's very strong.

BOY Uh, yeah.

OSCAR How much is the gentleman paying you?

BOY Five dollars.

OSCAR Oh, well then.

BOY That's a lot of money! And everything's all right. Nobody knows I'm here.

OSCAR I know you're here.

BOY Don't you want me to be here?

OSCAR At the moment I want to know why you are here.

BOY That old man said you would like me.

OSCAR And you would like me? Tell the truth.

BOY I would like the five dollars.

OSCAR Your eyes are red.

BOY I've been rubbing them.

OSCAR You've been crying.

BOY Uh, yes.

OSCAR Why?

BOY I'd rather not say.

OSCAR Five dollars.

BOY Somebody died.

OSCAR Who?

BOY I lost a friend.

OSCAR A waiter in the hotels or a bartender in the saloons or a cowboy on the plains? How old are you?

BOY I'm thirty.

OSCAR Please.

BOY Twenty-five.

OSCAR Not one penny.

BOY I'm eighteen.

OSCAR I hear most cowboys die of pneumonia more than gunfire. They are just that, boys. Is it true?

BOY I reckon.

OSCAR You're not a cowboy yourself?

BOY No.

OSCAR What are you?

BOY Not much.

OSCAR Smile. Have you ever gone to bed with a man before?

BOY Sure!

OSCAR Let me put that another way. Have you ever gone to bed with anyone before?

BOY Of course!

OSCAR Make it ten dollars. And tell me the truth.

BOY Women. Some.

OSCAR Do you want to go to bed with me?

BOY No.

OSCAR What do you want to do?

BOY Keep the ten dollars.

OSCAR You're in trouble.

BOY Yes.

OSCAR Are you afraid of someone?

BOY No.

OSCAR Steal something?

BOY No.

OSCAR Are you religious? Are you lamenting the crucifixion of Christ?

BOY No.

OSCAR Well then. Is your heart broken?

BOY Yes.

OSCAR Do you need five more dollars to tell me why?

BOY You won't care.

OSCAR Who knows?

BOY My sister died.

OSCAR Really?

BOY We grew up together. Now she's gone.

OSCAR When?

BOY Three days ago.

OSCAR Was there a funeral?

BOY There was a burial.

OSCAR Did you cry then?

BOY No.

OSCAR You should have. I did.

BOY What?

OSCAR Cry. When my sister died. We must, you know.

BOY You had a sister who died?

OSCAR I was twelve. She was ten. *(He takes a faded envelope from his pocket. It has childish scrawls and sketches of angels on it.)* In this envelope, which I keep with me always, is a lock of her hair. *(He shows it to the* BOY, *then puts it on the table.)* Do you want to cry now?

BOY Yes.

OSCAR Why don't you?

BOY I'm working!

OSCAR For five dollars.

BOY Ten now!

OSCAR To go to bed with me instead of crying about her.

BOY Yes!

OSCAR There is only one thing that matters. For those who really love, there is no help. None. We must do that for ourselves.

BOY How?

OSCAR Begin by crying.

BOY What was your sister's name?

OSCAR Isola. What was yours?

BOY Sally.

OSCAR To Sally and to Isola. *Tread lightly, she is near, under the snow. Speak gently, she can hear the daisies grow. All her bright golden hair tarnished with rust. She that was young and fair fallen to dust . . . Peace, peace, she cannot hear lyre or sonnet. All my life's buried here, heap earth upon it.*

(The BOY *tries to hold back his grief.)*

BOY What's a lyre?

OSCAR A harp.

BOY Oh. *(He breaks down and weeps.* OSCAR *waits a moment, then takes out a bill and puts it in the* BOY's *hand.)* This is a hundred dollars.

OSCAR Good night.

BOY Thank you. Thank you. You are a good and kind gentleman. I hope people always treat you the way you've treated me.

OSCAR That is a brilliant line for an exit. I will remember it when I write a play.

BOY Good night, sir.

*(*OSCAR *nods and sits staring ahead, drinking absinthe and looking at the*

envelope. Band music. The BOY *goes to the coat tree and becomes the* YOUNG GENTLEMAN. *He changes his clothes.)*

YOUNG GENTLEMAN Delirium, to wander in mind. Colorado and its suns and moons, the vast open United States dissolves into the steel confines of Reading Gaol, where, as a convicted felon, as a foul corruptor of boys, he must soak thick rope in oakum tar, his hands bleeding, his ear split open and festering, his spirit destroyed by shame and humiliation. His only success was *Salome*, in Paris, which he never saw. It was the most shocking play ever taken from the Scriptures, and the best. But now that fur-lined coat is on his mind. *(He takes* OSCAR's *fur-lined coat and replaces it with a shabby one. He puts it on* OSCAR.*)* He lost it when he went into prison. He could never find another one like it when he came out, and he regrets that, as his death rattle begins, as he lies—the ex-convict, the morally impure abuser of youth—rash-ridden on a deathbed in the Hotel D'Alsace, dying beyond his means, fighting to the death with his wallpaper.

*(*OSCAR *gets up and walks about. The* YOUNG GENTLEMAN *now becomes a very proper young Englishman, with an elegant coat and vest, pearl-gray trousers, gloves, hat, and cane. He sits at the table. French children sing "Sur le pont d'Avignon," the sound distorted.* OSCAR *waves to them and moves slowly to the table.)*

YOUNG ENGLISH GENTLEMAN Good afternoon.

OSCAR Hello.

YOUNG GENTLEMAN Mr. Melmoth?

OSCAR Yes.

YOUNG GENTLEMAN What a pleasant day.

OSCAR Perfectly charming.

YOUNG GENTLEMAN Perhaps a little chilly.

OSCAR The children warm it up.

YOUNG GENTLEMAN They were singing for you?

OSCAR For the Queen of England. Today is her birthday and they were given a little party in her honor.

YOUNG GENTLEMAN By you.

OSCAR Tea and cake. A few tiny gifts children like. Children make me forget.

YOUNG GENTLEMAN Like a good café.

OSCAR This isn't a good café. It is fifth-rate. With a very strange atmosphere, like something bizarre in a painting. But you seem intelligent. I approve that coat.

YOUNG GENTLEMAN I wanted to look my best.

OSCAR You are meeting someone important?

YOUNG GENTLEMAN Yes.

OSCAR Enjoy your friendships. They are as important to us as parties are to children. Are you French?

YOUNG GENTLEMAN No.

OSCAR You certainly aren't English. American?

YOUNG GENTLEMAN No.

OSCAR You remind me of—oh, many young gentlemen I knew. May I ask?

YOUNG GENTLEMAN I am from the East.

OSCAR No further questions but this one: Do you have any money?

YOUNG GENTLEMAN Do you want a drink?

OSCAR Yes, I *would* like a drink, yes.

YOUNG GENTLEMAN Then you must have one. On me.

OSCAR I am unable to return the favor.

YOUNG GENTLEMAN Quite all right. Ah, we're in luck. (*The* YOUNG GENTLEMAN *indicates the absinthe bottle and two glasses, still on the table.*) You drink absinthe, I think.

OSCAR Oh yes, absinthe, yes. I am very good company.

(*The* YOUNG GENTLEMAN *pours the green absinthe into the glasses.*)

YOUNG GENTLEMAN I thought you might be.

OSCAR Once, please believe this, I was thought the best dinner companion in the world. Now I sell its memory, the only currency I have. Of course, that was all in another country.

YOUNG GENTLEMAN England? Cheers.

OSCAR Cheers. *(They drink together.)* Ever been there?

YOUNG GENTLEMAN Once or twice.

OSCAR Did you like it?

YOUNG GENTLEMAN Some of it.

OSCAR But not all.

YOUNG GENTLEMAN Definitely not all.

OSCAR I can't go there anymore.

YOUNG GENTLEMAN I like the lawns and the cheerfulness.

OSCAR And the hard work.

YOUNG GENTLEMAN And the carols.

OSCAR Bookbinding.

YOUNG GENTLEMAN First-rate.

OSCAR Music?

YOUNG GENTLEMAN Some.

OSCAR Architecture?

YOUNG GENTLEMAN Not always.

OSCAR Bit chilling.

YOUNG GENTLEMAN Often.

OSCAR They get so angry sometimes. They did at me.

YOUNG GENTLEMAN Anger is not a productive state.

OSCAR Are you an artist?

YOUNG GENTLEMAN I do many things.

OSCAR Artists make nothing good out of hatred. They must love the world, no matter what it does to them.

YOUNG GENTLEMAN Or they to it.

OSCAR That is exceedingly well put.

YOUNG GENTLEMAN Thank you.

OSCAR I must say, you make me recall something I have not felt for a long time.

YOUNG GENTLEMAN What?

OSCAR Encouragement.

YOUNG GENTLEMAN I knew of a gentleman once who encouraged others. All the time. Would you like to hear about him?

OSCAR Gladly.

YOUNG GENTLEMAN This gentleman was very eloquent. He talked about Art.

OSCAR I hope he wasn't tiresome.

YOUNG GENTLEMAN No, he wasn't. He said there is no need to talk about reality. That just happens. But we must talk about Art, so it will exist. Otherwise we kill it. And that is a profound tragedy, since nature is always reproducing itself for its survival, but every real work of art is unique, created by one single person, who will never come again and is perfectly, beautifully useless. He illustrated this bizarre notion by telling stories about Jesus Christ, of all people, whom he considered not God but a perfectly realized and very great artist, whose art was his life. In one of his stories Christ comes across a drunken sinner, with roses in his hair, his lips red with wine, and says to him, "My friend, why do you live like this?" And the sinner says, "I was a leper. You healed me. I was so miserable then, I must be happy now."

(OSCAR smiles and nods.)

OSCAR Ah yes. Then Christ saw a woman with another sinner following her, and Christ said, "My friend, why are you looking at that woman that way?" and the sinner said, "I was blind and you healed me. What else should I do with my eyes?"

YOUNG GENTLEMAN And Christ saw a third man, crying, and he said, "My friend, why are you crying?" And the man said, "I was dead and you brought me back to life. What else should I do in this life but cry?"

OSCAR Then Christ was very sad. He went and sat next to His Father in heaven, where all these sinners stood naked in the Judgment Hall of God.

YOUNG GENTLEMAN "You have lived an evil life," said God the Father to a fourth sinner. "I must send you to hell."

OSCAR "You can't," said the fourth sinner.

YOUNG GENTLEMAN "Why not?" said God.

OSCAR "Because I always lived there," said the fourth sinner. And there was silence in the Judgment Hall of God.

YOUNG GENTLEMAN And Christ said, "Well, since you can't send him to hell, send him to heaven."

OSCAR "He can't do that either," said the fourth sinner.

YOUNG GENTLEMAN "Why not?" said Christ.

OSCAR "Because I have no art, and without art, I cannot imagine heaven."

YOUNG GENTLEMAN And Christ said to a fifth sinner, "Are you an artist, too?" And the fifth sinner said, "Yes," and Christ said to the fifth sinner, "How do you imagine God's heaven with your art?"

OSCAR The sinner said, "I am a sculptor. My wife died. I was desolate, and deathly ill. I made a status of myself mourning over her tomb. I called it *The Sorrow That Lasts Forever.* But it did not help. I thought I would go mad with grief. Nothing made any sense. So I broke it up. I made a statue of a dancer. I put it by the tomb, and I called it *The Pleasure That Lasts for a Moment.* And I saw heaven."

YOUNG GENTLEMAN And there was a great silence in the Judgment Hall of God.

(Pause.)

OSCAR Did we know each other? I don't remember telling you my stories anywhere.

YOUNG GENTLEMAN I was there, where you were. I did that, too, upon occasion. Tell stories, I mean.

OSCAR Why did you listen to mine?

YOUNG GENTLEMAN Like the sculptor who thinks in bronze, I think in stories. So do you.

OSCAR That is absolutely true. Who are you?

YOUNG GENTLEMAN Someone like you. *(A band softly plays "God Save the Queen."* OSCAR *stands, staring, stricken, but not showing it. The* YOUNG GENTLEMAN *drinks his absinthe. The band finishes.)*

YOUNG GENTLEMAN That is what they took away from you.

OSCAR Yes. Well.

YOUNG GENTLEMAN They don't like you.

OSCAR No.

YOUNG GENTLEMAN I do, though. More?

OSCAR Please. *(The* YOUNG GENTLEMAN *pours.)* You are a very curious gentleman.

YOUNG GENTLEMAN So are you.

OSCAR My name is not Melmoth.

YOUNG GENTLEMAN I know what your name is. Cheers.

OSCAR Cheers. *(They drink together.)* Really, we must have met. I do seem to remember you from somewhere.

YOUNG GENTLEMAN We've seen each other about. You with another young man.

OSCAR You've seen him? Here?

YOUNG GENTLEMAN Very beautiful, and very wicked.

OSCAR Do you know where he is now?

YOUNG GENTLEMAN I do.

OSCAR *Where??* Sorry. I raised my voice. That is what he does to me.

YOUNG GENTLEMAN I understand.

OSCAR I still love him.

YOUNG GENTLEMAN But does he love you?

OSCAR He tries. He comes to see me, then gets bored. I have no money. He calls me an old whore, and leaves me.

YOUNG GENTLEMAN He won't do that again.

OSCAR No?

YOUNG GENTLEMAN He inherited a fortune. He's raising horses.

OSCAR Horses?

YOUNG GENTLEMAN Um. Do you still love him?

OSCAR Forever.

YOUNG GENTLEMAN In spite of what he did to you?

OSCAR Or because of it. Do you understand what it is to be betrayed?

YOUNG GENTLEMAN It is a part of my charm, as it will be of yours.

OSCAR Then you've been betrayed, too?

YOUNG GENTLEMAN Once.

OSCAR You loved as strongly as I did?

YOUNG GENTLEMAN Oh, yes.

OSCAR Who?

YOUNG GENTLEMAN You, among others. I am very promiscuous that way.

OSCAR And were you betrayed as I was?

YOUNG GENTLEMAN I told you, once. But that once was spectacular.

OSCAR I am very drunk. This absinthe. You are so charming. Well, are you Jesus Christ?

YOUNG GENTLEMAN I am.

OSCAR This is absurd. Really?

YOUNG GENTLEMAN Positively, none other, I assure you.

OSCAR It would be just like me, when I lie dying, to presume I meet you, have known you somewhere before, when I loved the Gospels at Oxford, or perhaps here and there, some young man who looked like you.

YOUNG GENTLEMAN Does it matter, if it's me?

OSCAR No. In that case, how do you do?

YOUNG GENTLEMAN Very well, thank you.

OSCAR Why are you here, waiting for me?

YOUNG GENTLEMAN As the artist on his deathbed sees heaven, you see me.

OSCAR On my deathbed?

YOUNG GENTLEMAN Yes.

OSCAR Oh. Am I dead yet?

YOUNG GENTLEMAN Not quite.

OSCAR I hate to seem inquisitive, but when do I die?

YOUNG GENTLEMAN When you stop dreaming.

OSCAR You're being obscure. I see you quite clearly. We sit, talk. Dreams jump about.

YOUNG GENTLEMAN Not the last one. Death you of all men see as a story. This is your last story.

OSCAR Meeting Jesus in a fifth-rate café, is that a good story?

YOUNG GENTLEMAN I like it.

OSCAR Is this all there is to it?

YOUNG GENTLEMAN A friend will call a priest. You will raise your hand and be received into the Church. All perfectly natural. Another? *(He pours* OSCAR *another absinthe.)*

OSCAR Thank you so much. *(The* YOUNG GENTLEMAN *pours for himself. They drink.)* What will happen to my sons?

YOUNG GENTLEMAN One will try to forget you. He will be a soldier, die bravely in war. The other will remember you, live a long time, have a son of his own, who will have a son. They will write loving books about you.

OSCAR And I?

(The YOUNG GENTLEMAN *gets up, stands behind* OSCAR, *with his hands on* OSCAR's *shoulders.)*

YOUNG GENTLEMAN You will die in a fifth-rate hotel, like this café. That's where you are now. Only a few friends are with you, but they are doing their best. The owner of the poor hotel holds you in his arms. So do I.

OSCAR Why does he care? Why do you?

YOUNG GENTLEMAN Wouldn't it be boring if I came for the righteous?

OSCAR It would be tedious.

YOUNG GENTLEMAN Should not those who love more than most be forgiven more than most?

OSCAR That is perfectly charming. *(He coughs, grasps his throat.)* Oh! *(He breathes with terrible difficulty.)*

YOUNG GENTLEMAN It will only be a moment.

OSCAR I—can't—breathe!

YOUNG GENTLEMAN Then don't.

*(*OSCAR *dies, then breathes freely again.)*

OSCAR I feel so much better!

YOUNG GENTLEMAN Are you quite ready?

OSCAR Whenever you are.

YOUNG GENTLEMAN Then we'll go.

(He hands OSCAR *his hat and cane. They start off.)*

YOUNG GENTLEMAN Would you like to say goodbye?

OSCAR I beg your pardon?

(The YOUNG GENTLEMAN *indicates the audience.)*

YOUNG GENTLEMAN To the future.

OSCAR Oh, yes. *(Band music. The* YOUNG GENTLEMAN *nods, steps back, takes off his hat and waits. To the audience)* I lost my friends in life, but I hope to make new ones after death. I do so want you to be among them. You can easily find me. Where there is laughter and pleasure, there is truth. There I will wait for you. Good night.

(The YOUNG GENTLEMAN *puts on his hat, holds out his hand for* OSCAR *to join him.* OSCAR *does and, as the band plays softly, goes with him into Paradise.)*

Maiden Lane

'99

› CASSANDRA MEDLEY

ORIGINAL PRODUCTION

DIRECTOR Irving Vincent
SET DESIGNER Kris Stone
COSTUME DESIGNER Amela Baksic
SOUND Beatrice Terry
PROPS Erika Malone
PRODUCTION STAGE MANAGER Gretchen A. Knowlton
STAGE MANAGER Gail Eve Malatesta

The cast was as follows:
KATE Judy Tate
LEON Johnny Lee Davenport
EVELYN Judith Roberts
FRANCINE Petie Trigg Seale

CHARACTERS

KATE thirty-something, very light-skinned black woman who could pass for white

LEON Kate's husband, mid- to late thirties, dark-skinned

EVELYN a white woman in her sixties

FRANCINE Kate's mother, fifty; a very light-skinned black woman

PLACE

Kate and Leon's house on Taylor Avenue
Evelyn's house on Maiden Lane
Kate and Leon's car

TIME

Spring, 1999

NOTE

Stage setting is minimal, created by the lighting, and with minimal props. A simple seating unit converts from a couch into a bed and then into the front seat of a car.

KATE *and* LEON's *kitchen. As the lights come up, they are already talking as they cook: chopping, slicing, stirring a simmering pot.*

LEON . . . Maiden Lane? Lemme get this straight. You mean the *real* Maiden Lane?

KATE Maiden Lane. Right on the lakeside there. Overlooking Maiden Lake.

LEON I gotta see this. *(Reaching for object.)* Hand me the lemons. *(She does. He slices them.)* Bay leaves, what'd I do with the bay leaves . . .

KATE Listen, it's exactly—it's positively everything we want. Everything we've been holding out for.

(EVELYN enters her own pool of light on the opposite side of the stage. She motions as if showing a room.)

EVELYN Full-size patio deck. And my late husband and I built in the Jacuzzi . . .

KATE *(To LEON, as if recounting to him)* . . . Jacuzzi . . . patio—full-sized, by the way, and overlooking the lake. Lake. Lake. Lake.

LEON I like it—I like it.

EVELYN *(Continuing as if KATE is standing beside her)* This is the sunroom or breakfast nook. Dining room is through here, and you'll see the kitchen is redone with handmade tiles . . . Lovely, yes? He's a Native American artist in Santa Fe. The study through here . . .

KATE *(To LEON)* . . . And this kitchen, baby. Fully outfitted, renovated, opens onto the patio, skylight over the cupboards. You can "gourmet" down, suga. *(She kisses him.)*

EVELYN *(Continuing)* . . . Sunken den with bay windows . . .

KATE *(To LEON)* . . . On three sides . . . and get this . . .

EVELYN And fireplaces in the den, the living room . . . and the master bedroom "suite" . . .

(KATE and LEON slap palms.)

LEON Let's move in tomorrow.

KATE And get this . . .

EVELYN . . . and here's the . . . whirlpool . . .

KATE *(To LEON)* Plus this whirlpool in the master bathroom.

EVELYN *(As if addressing an unseen person)* Now that my husband's gone, I just want to move back to Santa Fe permanently. *(She disappears.)*

KATE So far she's seen just two other couples—but—but—wait, wait, I'm telling you, she and I—just, y'know, clicked. I can feel it. This is a fantastic, amazing place . . .

LEON Hey, I believe you.

KATE . . . Set back from the road—pines on three sides . . . then that wide blue water . . .

LEON *(As he stirs the pot)* Two couples ahead. *(He offers her a taste of the sauce simmering in the pot.)* Two "white" couples ahead.

(She is silent, and doesn't taste the simmering sauce. He tastes it instead.)

KATE *(Matter-of-factly)* Well, naturally.

(LEON holds out the spoon to her. She tastes and makes a face.)

LEON Still too tart?

(Pause. KATE nods, then moves on.)

KATE Look, baby . . .

LEON Nono—let's backtrack here a bit. Now, your lunch hour, right? And you decide to strike out on your own . . .

KATE Not "on my own." Don't make it sound so—y'know . . . It wasn't like that. Intentional or something. Don't make it sound so . . . Look, I had an impulse. And two hours free for lunch. Decided to see what might happen.

LEON *(Stirring pot and tasting, adding spices.)* Ummm-umm.

KATE Look, none of these damn realtors show us the whole list.

LEON That's just a given.

KATE Right. So this afternoon I thought, Why not try and best them at their own game. See the full lay of the land for once. So I paid a call on Casey and Evans—over in the Northland Mall.

(Silence.)

LEON Ginger. Where's the ginger . . .

(Silence.)

KATE I mean, I figured, since I have the means to fool . . .

LEON Without me you *do* "have the means."

KATE Forget it—forget it!

LEON Wait wait—what? It's just a fact, that's all.

KATE If you're gonna make it sound so calculated . . . and get so—
so . . .

LEON So, what? What?

KATE Fine. Let's keep looking. The place on Holland Drive—I'm
not opposed to it—if that's what you wanna settle with, fine.

LEON Who's talking settling? Dang.

(Silence.)

KATE God Almighty, it was just an experiment, okay?

LEON Great, let's check it out together, then. See what she's got to
say when she sees us. Together.

KATE Okay. Fine. Great. *(*LEON *continues to stir the pot, sprinkling in a
few more ingredients. She opens a bottle of wine, watching him, then
moves over and kisses him.)* It was just one of my crazy-ass, spur-of-
the-moment whims, y'know.

LEON *(Lovingly)* Just like you to throw up your hands and do something off-the-wall like that.

(They both laugh.)

KATE *(Shrugs.)* I figured, Hey, lemme just walk in and let 'em assume what they probably are gonna automatically assume anyway. Next thing I know, they're showing me Maiden Lane.

(Silence.)

LEON Swam across it once. On a dare.

KATE What?

LEON Yep. Maiden Lake. At midnight. Way back in high school.
Me, Frenchy, Dante, Tyrone, my partners-in-crime.

KATE Y'all were desperate for some jail time, huh?

LEON *(Laughs.)* Hey, we badass boys from the Projects took off, high on Boone's Farm Apple Wine . . .

KATE No . . . !

LEON *(Nodding.)* Drove all the way out there, snuck up on somebody's, y'know, "spread" . . . Dove in, man. Swam clear 'cross that sucker and back.

KATE Stupid and dangerous.

LEON Kids.

KATE *(Wryly)* And this was after Princeton let you in, or before?

LEON *(A moment.)* Don't remember. *(He finishes stirring.)* Ready to pour. (KATE *reaches her finger in to taste. He stops her.*) Unh-unh. First gotta sprinkle in the you-know-what.

(They grab each other and kiss passionately. She breaks away, he grabs her back.)

KATE *(Playfully)* Hey, I'm hungry.

LEON D'you love me for myself or for my sauce?

KATE *(Laughing.)* Believe me, you don't wanna know.

(Pause.)

LEON Look. Okay. *(Pause.)* Say you test this woman. (KATE *stops, stares at him.*) I mean, only if you want to. It's up to you. I mean, if you think it's too weird . . . *(Stops.)* In fact, forget it. It's too weird.

KATE Nono, wait. Wait. *(Pause.)* It would just be an experiment. Period. We find out whatever— Then that's that, we move on, case closed. *(Pause.)* Okay?

(They stare at each other. Lights cross-fade into the next day.)

(EVELYN's house. KATE moves over to EVELYN's area of the stage. EVELYN enters, tea tray in hand, with pot and cups and photos of EVELYN's house. KATE sits rather stiffly, formally.)

EVELYN Here we are—Earl Grey and scones.

KATE Thanks for seeing me again.

EVELYN Cream? My husband and I put a lot of years into this place. I prefer to interview people myself.

KATE Naturally.

EVELYN Too bad your husband can't be here to see the place.

KATE It's possible he could be back soon. Depends . . . *(She picks up the photos from the tray.)* . . . on his clients. Meanwhile, with your permission, I'll fax him these. Give him a look at your beautiful home . . .

EVELYN Listen, I did my tour of duty as the corporate wife, my dear. I know only too well.

(An object catches KATE's *eye.)*

KATE That vase . . .

EVELYN You may take a closer look, if you wish.

KATE It's so—

EVELYN Yes?

KATE This glaze. Opaque and translucent, both.

EVELYN Ummm.

*(*EVELYN *suddenly notices something out of the window that faces the audience. She takes out a pair of binoculars and raises them to her eyes, gazing out toward the audience, that is, toward the lake.* KATE *stands beside her, also gazing out.)*

KATE *(Admiring, pointing.)* That's quite a schooner.

*(*EVELYN *hands* KATE *the binoculars.* KATE *looks out, reading the name of the passing boat.)*

EVELYN *(Indicating the boat.)* Wally McCallister, three houses down.

KATE *(Reading through binoculars.)* The Sinbad.

EVELYN He's not a subtle man.

*(*KATE *hands the binoculars to* EVELYN, *begins to continue looking at the photos—but is drawn to the vase.)*

KATE It's like the glaze is floating, hovering on the surface.

EVELYN *(Curtly)* Very true.

KATE Are there others?

EVELYN You're holding the only one of its kind. (KATE *stares at* EVELYN.) What?

KATE It's yours.

EVELYN Of course it's mine.

KATE You know what I mean. You're the artist. Aren't you?

EVELYN *(Rather brusque)* Perhaps.

KATE *(Sincerely)* It's good. Really. *(Pause. She self-consciously resumes gazing out the window, and points.)* They seem to be having quite a good time out there.

EVELYN Oh, Wally entertains all kinds of clients during the week. One of the many benefits of living on a lake.

KATE Lovely.

(EVELYN *continues to look through the binoculars, then indicates to* KATE.)

EVELYN The . . . ah . . . folks to the left . . .

KATE *(Looking.)* The black couple.

EVELYN Not residents. Guests.

KATE *(Pause.)* Right.

EVELYN *(Pointing out the window.)* Ah, here comes my hummingbird to feed, right on schedule. More tea?

(KATE *turns, walks into* LEON's *area of the stage.*)

(*Night.* KATE *and* LEON's *bedroom. They are undressing. She has just told him about* EVELYN's *comment.*)

LEON *(Nodding.)* Well well well . . .

KATE Yep. *(Pause.)*

LEON "Guests."

KATE She wanted to reassure me.

LEON Ha.

KATE And how was your day?

LEON Oh, great. Guess who's set to design the Jamison Plaza complex.

KATE *(Hopeful)* Honey?

LEON *(Self-mockingly)* In your dreams. Byron "invited" Steve to a sushi lunch and handed it to him. To him.

KATE But your seniority!

LEON Naw-naw . . . I'm only good for designing "affordable housing." After all, I'm more in "touch" with the "hood"—with the people on the street.

KATE They said that?

LEON Katie, do they have to *say* it?

KATE *(Soothing him)* Baby—

LEON Oh, now, when the Knicks and the Bulls are at the Garden, then it's—*(Makes a mocking high-five.)* Leon, let's go for a round on the house. *(Pause.)* But when it comes to the circle within the circle . . .

KATE You hang tough and study the target. You'll get there. Remember, you've got a "queen" in your corner. *(She kisses his hand.)*

(Kissing her, LEON *takes the remote. Soft music rises.)*

LEON Hey, let's just lock out the world . . . kick back . . . and relax. *(Sexy)* Maybe try some extracurricular activity. *(As they caress they begin to passionately make love, when suddenly* LEON *grabs her in his arms, holding her. A mocking afterthought)* "Guests"!

KATE Wanna claim it?

LEON The house?

KATE We could. *(Pause. She kisses him. He stops. They stare at each other. Lights cross-fade.)*

(EVELYN's house. KATE *and* LEON's *house. The next evening.* LEON *remains on his side of the stage, setting down his briefcase, removing his tie, as if*

home from a long day. He addresses KATE *as if she is standing right in front of him.* KATE *turns and speaks to him when necessary, otherwise remains beside* EVELYN, *inside* EVELYN'S *space. She points to a painting hanging on the invisible stage wall.)*

KATE . . . of all the paintings in the house. This one. Amber slashing into ocher—great. And having this right at the window—it can kind of glow along with the lake.

*(*LEON *applauds* KATE.*)*

LEON Go, girl—talk the talk.

KATE *(To* LEON*)* Thing is, she really *is* good.

LEON All the better, so you won't have to fake it.

EVELYN *(Referring to the painting)* Wanted to try for something that could blend with dusk. Decades of evenings I've spent in this spot. *(Pause.)* Staring out.

KATE *(To* EVELYN*)* It's acrylic base, right?

EVELYN *(Nodding.)* They of course dry faster . . .

*(*LEON *calls out to* KATE *as she remains in* EVELYN'S *space.)*

LEON Did you check the drainage and the sewage system?

KATE *(To* EVELYN*)* Yes, it is a hypnotic view. I can see your inspiration.

LEON Did you ask her about flooding—basement flooding?

KATE *(Turning to him but remaining beside* EVELYN.*)* Yes yes yes.

LEON 'Cause, we not investing in no house with possible seasonal flooding. *(Referring to a list in his hand)* Did you—ask about . . . soil erosion? And rain gutters. Half the list is not checked off, Kate.

KATE *(Crosses over to his space and looks over the list in his hand.)* I'll get to it tomorrow.

LEON You couldn't get to it today?

KATE Patience, baby. Patience. Lemme concentrate on our rapport.

LEON Un-huh. As long as the "rapport" includes when the shutters were last replaced.

KATE *(Returns to* EVELYN'S *area, points at another painting.)* The black in this little one's so restful.

EVELYN Took years to get that one right. Make the shadow in it here—read "rest." Not "gloom."

KATE Not menace.

EVELYN Exactly.

KATE *(Studying* EVELYN.*)* So. Why'd you quit? Did you quit? *(Pulls back, embarrassed.)* Sorry, none of my business.

EVELYN *(Studies* KATE.*)* Why didn't *you* even start? Did you start?

KATE *(Balking.)* Wait wait . . .

EVELYN *(Interrupting, laughing, playful)* Too late! I've caught you!

KATE *(Pause.)* Maybe.

EVELYN So. *(Pause.)* You wanted to?

KATE *(Smiles.)* Well . . . y'know . . . "dabble". . .

EVELYN Oh, c'mon now—you take art much more seriously.

KATE *(Pause.)* An MBA in finance is more practical in the nineties.

EVELYN Ah. But the old "knot on the heart" remains.

(A long stare between the women. KATE *breaks the spell of* EVELYN'S *gaze with a cordial, dismissive, self-mocking wave of her hand. She steps out of* EVELYN'S *light and into* LEON'S. EVELYN *disappears.)*

(Moonlight from a window, night. KATE *and* LEON *are on the couch. She is using a small pad to sketch him.)*

KATE *(Reporting to* LEON*)* Probably was quoting her shrink. She's just the type.

LEON How do you know?

KATE What?

LEON What type she is. She's just a stranger—could be anybody . . .

KATE My impression, sweetheart— Just reporting what she said, that's all.

LEON *(Pause.)* Tonight let's do dinner under the covers.

KATE Ummm. Great.

LEON It's Tunisian Curried Lamb with a cumin-fennel glaze, and asparagus soufflé.

(LEON crosses into the kitchen. KATE continues to sketch him.)

KATE *(Laughing.)* How do you do it? Hm? I mean, the last thing I wanna do when I drag in after work is run three miles and *then* face a cookbook. And the more complicated the recipe, the better.

(LEON chops a small amount of herbs.)

LEON Well now, running's my release . . . the kitchen's my meditation . . . and the bed is . . .

(Pause.)

KATE Keep talking . . . keep talking.

LEON *(Smiling.)* Did you tell Evelyn what a gourmet I am— when not in London, Zurich—or wherever? *(Pause.)* Actually, where am I exactly?

KATE Cute. And no. She . . . Look, I don't go there to discuss my private life.

LEON *Right. (Pause.) Do* you miss it?—the old avant-garde— Kate?

KATE *(Dismissive)* Plea-se! Dragging my tail from gallery to gallery. Doors slammed in my face? Living on Chinese fried rice takeout and tossing canvases not worth looking at twice?

(KATE tears out the pages she has been drawing. He attempts to look; she crumples them before he can.)

LEON Tomorrow, don't forget to have her clarify the zoning regulations.

KATE Darling—

LEON 'Case we *do* decide to add a guest room over the garage. And the private dock, see if owners are allowed to extend it.

KATE Darling, I don't need instructions. *(Moving off.)* I'll set the table.

(LEON grabs her hand.)

LEON This is a major investment in our life together. *Together.*

(KATE takes his other hand.)

KATE Yes. "Yes."

(Lights cross-fade.)

(EVELYN's house—the dock. Sounds of water lapping against the dock. Lights show the reflection of the water. KATE and EVELYN sip coffee. They sit in lawn chairs, holding their faces up to the sun, wearing sunglasses and sunning themselves.)

EVELYN She's my cousin Gladys. She's set me up. Calls me last night to say she promised her daughter-in-law that I'll interview them for the house just as soon as they fly in from Seattle.

KATE Well, I can understand. I mean, family.

EVELYN *(Dismissively)* It's the old tale of "possible property brings forth long-lost kin." But I'm not giving them any special, privileged consideration.

(KATE settles back in her chair.)

KATE I'd live right here on this dock every day in summer.

EVELYN Ha. Dive in. Swim. Out. Tan. Back in, swim. Out. Tan. The kids used to —*(Stops herself.)* Never mind.

KATE No, what?

EVELYN *(Attempting to be dismissive)* Ah, now that I'm leaving, the old nostalgia bug is having its way with me.

KATE *(Sympathetically)* Did you teach your kids to swim off here?

EVELYN *(Nods. Demonstrates.)* Jamie, now tuck in your tummy, hold your breath, be brave now . . .

KATE and **EVELYN** Leap!

EVELYN Maiden Lane's an excellent place to bring up children. Award-winning school district—er—that is, if—

KATE Oh yes, that's part of the plan, as soon as I get my promotion.

EVELYN Ah, you younger women these days: marriage, motherhood, high finance, "liberation." *(Pause. Leaning in toward* KATE.*)* My third one was conceived on a skinny-dipping mission one moonlit night.

(They giggle. KATE *leafs through a portfolio lying on her lap. She refers to one of the drawings.)*

KATE What a face.

EVELYN *(Leaning over, looking.)* Her boyfriend was breaking up with her right there in the café.

KATE Seems like she's choking on a scream.

EVELYN *(Nods.)* And there I was, across the room, spying, and drawing away. She saw me, I just kept going. Gawd, I was so bold . . . so arrogant in those days.

KATE *(Pauses.)* My draftsmanship never got this good.

EVELYN Did it have a chance to? *(Pause.)* I'd love to see your work sometime.

KATE Nono, I—*(She can't find the words. She pantomimes ripping up paper and tossing it into the air.)*

EVELYN Kate! No. Not *all* of it?

*(*KATE *turns to* EVELYN. *They stare at each other. Lights cross-fade.)*

(Night. KATE *and* LEON'S. *They are reading through illustrated real-estate brochures.)*

LEON But the one in Sherwood Forest has a much smaller kitchen than the one in Troy Hills . . .

KATE But Troy Hills is so prefab-looking, you said so yourself.

LEON The Sherwood Forest one has the fireplace in the master bedroom.

KATE Yeah, that's a plus. And the living room's wider—opens right into the—

LEON But then we could just build a fireplace in the Troy Hills house.

KATE The Troy Hills houses all look like Xeroxes of the same style—we'll feel like "cyber clones" in that place.

LEON Hey now, we're too "hot" to clone, baby. Don't you know that? *(They nuzzle each other.)* At least both neighborhoods are integrated.

KATE Exactly.

LEON *(Caressing her.)* And great school systems when the time comes to look for schools.

KATE What's on the menu tonight, chef-of-my-heart? *(Pause. She realizes he is staring at her.)* Whatsamatter? *(Pause.)* What?

(Silence. LEON crosses into the kitchen and she follows. He begins chopping vegetables.)

LEON You don't really wanna give it up, do ya?

KATE Oh Lord—can we just please have one night, just one, without Maiden Lane coming up?

LEON Did you tell her you've decided to look elsewhere?

KATE I'm not gonna spoil my evening on this. I'm not.

LEON . . . or did you leave it open?

KATE I'm to call her tomorrow morning. Okay? And by that time her damn cousin'll probably have taken it. End of discussion.

LEON *(Pause.)* And if she hasn't . . .

KATE *(Interrupting quietly)* Please shut up about it.

LEON Answer me, Kate.

KATE We are not driving ourselves nuts over this, do you hear me?

LEON *(Pause.)* All right, then. You call her tomorrow . . . Tell her we decided no.

KATE *(Pause.)* Yes. *(She pours herself some wine.)*

(Silence.)

LEON *(Quietly)* Goddammit. *Fuck.*

KATE You want it as much as I do, don't you? Just for once, admit it.

LEON It's a buzz in my brain, I can't get the fucker out.

KATE There now, you see? Why should we let their not wanting us restrict our choice? Our "fear" guarantee their . . . their satisfaction? It's like bending 'cause they say Bend.

LEON Man man . . . okay. Yes.

KATE It's outrageous.

LEON Damnit all.

KATE Now you can buy into the very same turf where they threw you pennies to clip their hedges.

LEON *(Considers.)* Anyway, one day somebody black, Latin, whatever, is gonna break in there. One day. Shell-shock 'em, anyway . . .

KATE . . . and it might as well be us.

LEON I guess.

KATE She's invited me to lunch, actually.

LEON *(Whirls on her.)* Why didn't you tell me that to begin with?

KATE I said I'd phone first. No need if the cousin . . .

LEON Why, Kate?

KATE It's just a tentative invitation. You're taking this much too seriously.

LEON Am I? *(Pause.)* So now we're lunching, are we?

KATE Darling, you're acting like I've taken a lover. Stop it. *(Gestures with two fingers.)* We're this close, this close. *(Pause.)* Look, I see you. What you're . . . going through.

LEON Do you?

KATE Well, I love you, don't I? Of course. *(Silence.)* And I know I'm pretending. With her. It's my trick. I'm gaming her— And I'm clear. Totally clear.

LEON *(Pause.)* Even if we get it, it won't be over, y'know. They're not the cross-burning types, but they'll wall us in. Scorn us.

KATE *(Pause.)* Of course. That's exactly the "cold sweat" that they count on, isn't it?

LEON Breed the fear into the undesirables in the first place . . . And they'll keep themselves out.

KATE Are we gonna cave in?

(A pause as LEON *considers, then decides. He grabs a sealed bottle of wine, hands it to her.)*

LEON Tell her "hello" from your husband in London.

(They kiss. KATE *crosses into* EVELYN's *space.)*

(Afternoon. EVELYN's *house. A doorbell chimes.* EVELYN *comes up behind* KATE, *who jumps, startled.* EVELYN *carries an oblong two-foot-square box and some canvas board.)*

EVELYN Sorry. I was back in the garage.

KATE Ah. How are you today, Evelyn?

EVELYN How are you, Katherine?

KATE Fine. Great. Brought us a Bordeaux. *(She holds up a bottle of wine.)*

EVELYN *(Takes the wine bottle.)* Splendid. *(They enter the light, crossing to the table.* EVELYN *lays down the oblong box she is carrying.)* Decisions, decisions. What to save. What to throw out. I want to take nothing. I want to take everything.

KATE And I'm the same way.

EVELYN Except that you're at the starting gate, more or less, whereas I . . . *(She opens the box—she and* KATE *eye the old dried-up* *paint tubes. Waving away dust.)* My old friends. *(She fingers the tubes. Holds them up, speaks to them.)* Hi, there, remember me? Thought I'd croaked, didn't ya? *(To* KATE*)* Twenty. No, thirty years . . . all packed away. *(Stops herself.)* No. Excuse me, pardon me. I really must get past this godawful nostalgia nonsense!

*(*KATE *pats her hand ever so slightly.)*

KATE It's all right.

EVELYN All my cadmium yellow's used up.

*(*KATE *stares at the tubes. She can't help herself, and reaches down into the box. They stare at each other, smiling. Lights cross-fade.)*

(Evening. KATE *and* LEON'*s house.* FRANCINE *stands beside* LEON. *She is dressed stylishly and is handing him a champagne glass.* KATE *crosses back over to them, and they all raise their glasses high.)*

FRANCINE To the house!

KATE AND LEON The house.

LEON We still have to sign on the dotted line. Nothing's certain till the actual closing.

*(*FRANCINE *looks over the snapshots as* KATE *proudly points.)*

FRANCINE My pretty baby is now residing on the lakeshore at 8713 Maiden Lane.

KATE Just wait till you see this place for real—oh, just wait!!

FRANCINE Let's drive out there now—what do you say!

LEON Ha. It's gonna still be there when we finish dinner, Momma Francine.

KATE *(Interrupting)* It's so late, you won't be able to see it really in the dark . . . *(To* LEON*)* Right, hon?

FRANCINE We could take a quick spin—

KATE Quick? No, no, Momma. *(Playful)* When you lay your eyes on our new Shangri-la, I want you to get the full effect and be able to take your time doing it.

FRANCINE But this would be my prevue of coming attractions.

KATE Darling, I wish we *could*, I really wish we could. Lee has to get up so early. As a matter-of-fact, that makes two of us. I've got this monthly strategy breakfast at my office tomorrow. *(Pause.)* Hey now, we're having Lee's famous lemon swordfish tonight. What do you want to drink, Mom—white or red.

FRANCINE You know me, m'dear. Martini first, before all, and always. *(To* LEON*)* Lee, what was your impression of the woman when she finally confirmed the sale?

LEON Me? I wasn't there.

KATE He couldn't get off work.

FRANCINE *(To* LEON*)* Darlin', I know you hated that.

LEON *(Staring at* KATE.*)* You don't know how much.

FRANCINE *(To* LEON*)* Otherwise, though, she *does* know you.

KATE Are you kidding, she was charmed the moment she met him.

*(*LEON *regards* KATE.*)*

LEON Oh, yeah. The minute . . . she met me.

FRANCINE *(To* LEON*)* Is that so?

*(*LEON *gives a quick, stressed smile.)*

LEON The fish. *(He exits.)*

KATE I tell you, when she confirmed the sale, my heart just leaped over. *(Mixing the martini.)* Of course, she's a very liberal type—

FRANCINE Ah— Well. Good. Too bad your neighbors won't be.

*(*LEON *stands in the kitchen entryway watching them, tension building the more he hears.)*

KATE We won't get the burning crosses. They'll snub us, keep us out of the country club. Well, that's money we'll just save.

*(*FRANCINE *turns to* LEON.*)*

FRANCINE Lee, I wanna hear from you on this. What amazes me is that the realtors showed you two the place to begin with.

KATE *(Jumping in)* Now, that's where we lucked out. We found the exception to the rule on that, didn't we, honey?

(A pause as FRANCINE *looks from* LEON *to* KATE.*)*

LEON Um-hum. *(Stiff)* We found the exception, all right. We sure did.

KATE We're gonna throw a big ole housewarming party, string lights down to the dock.

FRANCINE Katie sweetie, I'll help. I'll even force myself to be in the same room with "that woman."

KATE Momma, Charlene is Daddy's second wife.

FRANCINE *(Pause.)* But to think that you two walk in, gorgeous as you are, and they take one look at you—and—and they still show you this particular place.

LEON I hope everybody's hungry.

FRANCINE *(To* LEON*)* Did you think it strange at first, Leon? Knowing you, you probably were suspicious, huh?

KATE *(Jumping in)* Frankly, I think the woman must have been firm with the company. She obviously told them she'd show her place to—you know—anybody who could afford to buy. I mean, you know, times have changed, not everywhere, but in this particular case, well, there you are.

FRANCINE *(Playfully, to* KATE*)* Darlin', let Mr. Leon the Lion get a word in, please. *(To* LEON*)* Sure are mighty quiet this evening.

LEON I'll set the table in the dining room, guys.

FRANCINE *(To* LEON*)* Don't you want to jump for joy?

(A pause as they wait for LEON *to speak. Suddenly* KATE *drops a kitchen implement to the floor.)*

KATE Oops. Sorry. *(To* FRANCINE*)* So excited. 'Member how I used to get on Christmas Eve?

FRANCINE *(To* LEON*)* What I can't get over is—

KATE Thing is, my honey's so tired, it's been a long week. You know, at work and all.

LEON *(Pause. To* FRANCINE*)* Yep. It sure has been. A *long* week.

FRANCINE *(Kissing* KATE*'s cheek.)* All I know is, my baby takes after me. And she would never use "this"—*(Indicates their skin color.)* To take advantage or to get ahead . . . *(To* LEON*)* Now, of course, Kate's daddy, on the other hand . . .

KATE Momma, don't. Please.

FRANCINE *(To* LEON*)* Stanley and his whole side of the family's always using "shade" to— Well, why bore you with the details.

(LEON *offers* FRANCINE *a wineglass.)*

LEON Now, this Chardonnay's Australian, Momma Francine, what you think?

FRANCINE *(Pressing on)* . . . But not us McClellans from North Carolina! Never. We've always held that if you can't win one for the race with a clean fight, then you haven't really won.

LEON Uh. Uh-huh. There's extra shitake-lemon sauce for anybody who wants it.

FRANCINE *(To* LEON*)* Frankly, that's why my father didn't want me to marry Stanley in the first place. Now, colored had to sit upstairs at the movies when I came along. And m'daddy always made sure we joined the other Negroes up there. Proudly. With the rest of our people. Proud. But when I met Stan—

KATE *(Interrupting* FRANCINE*)* Guess what? We painted today, Momma. How 'bout that?

FRANCINE Who painted?

(KATE *drapes herself with a paint-splattered kitchen apron as she speaks.* EVELYN *stands in her separate space, putting on a paint-splattered kitchen apron, picking brushes out of the oblong box.* LEON *stares at* KATE. FRANCINE *stares straight out at the audience, as if picturing the scene that*

KATE *describes. Whenever* KATE *addresses* FRANCINE *or* LEON, EVELYN *does not acknowledge or hear this, but mimes painting an invisible canvas.)*

EVELYN *(As if* KATE *is standing beside her)* Just smearing it on, I feel twenty years younger . . .

FRANCINE *(Laughing. To* KATE*)* Who would've thought that your messing around in paints would one day pay off. *(Pause. To* LEON*)* What's the kitchen like in the new house, Lee?

*(*KATE *and* LEON *lock eyes as* KATE *moves into* EVELYN's *space.)*

EVELYN *(To* KATE *re the canvas)* Start in anywhere. Don't impose definition. Let your hand take charge. *(*KATE *and* EVELYN *mime painting imaginary canvases, side by side.)* How's the word from London?

KATE *(Painting.)* Oh . . . the deal is smooth sailing. Lee's clients are pleased, so he's pleased.

EVELYN Bet he's handsome. *(Refers to* KATE's *painting)* Did you really want to smudge out that red?

KATE *(Studies her painting.)* Well . . . actually, no. *(Painting)* Actually I think I want lots of red—red and red and red.

EVELYN Then have it! Free up. Use the palette knife. Is he?

KATE *(Painting.)* Mmm?

EVELYN Handsome? *(Pause.)* Darryl was handsome.

KATE Oh, I can see that.

EVELYN Any photos of Lee?

KATE Er . . . wrong purse, too bad. *(Then playfully)* But he "turns heads."

EVELYN Tell me, what kind of art do you collect?

KATE Well, my stuff is mostly—er—y'know . . . *(Pause.)* Oceanic. *(Pause.)* Some Native American. *(Pause.)* Some African.

EVELYN Ah, the tribal— The walls would be hanging with masks and bright patterned cloth . . . weavings . . .

KATE *(Uneasy—has she said the wrong thing?)* Well . . . I'm not— I mean, decorating this place would be entirely different from my place on Taylor Avenue.

EVELYN No, I like the idea of "tribal" taking over when I'm gone. *(Pause.)* It's yours, by the way. Say hello to your new house.

(KATE turns to FRANCINE and LEON.)

KATE *(To FRANCINE)* We shook on it and the FOR SALE sign's coming down.

(FRANCINE raises her glass in a toast.)

FRANCINE Well, well. Here's to God's blessings and to paint. *(Pause.)* But I still can't get over how you got them to show y'all that house . . .

(Lights fade on them as LEON stares at KATE. FRANCINE continues talking.)

(Moonlight. The sound of chirping crickets. The road across from EVELYN's house. KATE and LEON sit in their car, side by side, LEON at the steering wheel. KATE pulls out a pair of binoculars, looks out at the audience through the lens as if gazing at a distant sight. Silence.)

KATE *All right.* Before you boil over—

LEON Lying to that bitch across the road there is one thing. But lying to the family—to Francine—

KATE Will you just, just please, please, look it over. *(She hands him the binoculars. He raises them to his eyes, looks.)* We'll plant rhodies, and mums along the driveway there . . . That's the breakfast nook on the right . . . then the dining room . . . Patio you can't see, but it wraps around the . . . *(Pause. She kisses his hand, places it on her breast.)* Here's where we're gonna give "little one" a second chance . . . *(Silence.)* It'll be ours. We won't have to sneak out here in the dark.

(LEON is silent.)

LEON Y'mean you won't have to sneak *me* out.

KATE Why don't you be up front and just say you don't want to do this—

LEON *Me* be up front?

KATE *(Sighs.)* Turn the car around, let's go home.

LEON *Don't pretend you agree to give it up.* Don't fucking do that.

KATE You just stop it. Stop brooding like I'm a bad little girl who needs her hands slapped. Jesus!

LEON *(Mocking)* Yeah, we better call on *somebody.*

KATE Be sarcastic. Do you really wanna back down now that we have it? Tell me the truth.

LEON Have you been telling *me* the truth?

KATE Oh, c'mon, buster. You're drooling over this.

(LEON *looks through the binoculars, then snatches them away from his face.*)

LEON Oh, it's beautiful. Yeah. It's a turn-on, all right. After all, I'm the up-and-coming, three-piece-suited "brotha" on the way up. *(Sarcastically)* And up and up and up!! *(Pause.)* Yes! Yes, I want my boss to salivate when I tell him I'm moving to Maiden Lane. Yes. *(Pause.)* And I can just picture m'daddy fishing from our dock, nodding and giving me the ole "Well done, son" pat on the back. Oh, yes. *(Pause.)* It scratches my itch for the finer things in life, God help me.

KATE Can't we just enjoy the fact that it's ours? We won.

LEON What did we win, Katie? Why didn't you tell me you painted?

KATE What does that matter?

LEON What else haven't you told me?

KATE Nothing.

LEON *(Seething quietly)* What. Else. Happened.

KATE *(Straining for patience)* She shook my hand. She called her bank. Done deal.

LEON *Stop bullshitting me.*

KATE *It's none of your goddamn business.*

LEON Wanna trash this marriage, baby? Your call.

(Silence. He waits, then turns on the ignition, starts to turn the car around. A beat, sound of the car tires turning around. KATE *suddenly stays his hand.)*

KATE *(Suddenly—a floodgate bursting)* Hold me!! *Hold me.*

(He stares at her as . . . Lights up on EVELYN'S *space.* KATE *returns to the space. They mime painting imaginary canvases, side by side.)*

EVELYN No, I like the idea of "tribal" taking over when I'm gone.
(Pause.) It's yours, by the way. Say hello to your new house.

*(*KATE *stops, stares at* EVELYN, *speechless.)*

KATE But—er—the other couples—and your cousin's niece?

*(*EVELYN *dismisses this with a wave of her hand.)*

EVELYN Plebeians.

KATE *(Delighted)* Wonderful. Fantastic. Gawd, I've been, we've been looking for so long—and the lake—to be able to live by such a wonderful— Thank you. Thank you.

EVELYN Start painting again. For me. Would you do that?

KATE Well, I—*(Stops. Floored.)*

EVELYN Hosting a dinner party— Thirty, forty years ago now. For Darryl's clients. *(Holds up her hands, palms up, as if examining them.)* Couldn't get the blue off in time to serve the veal scallopini, or whatever nonsense it was. Darryl and the guests arrive and there I am, paint-covered—fingernails encrusted with blue.

KATE Well, just apologize. Serve drinks. Go change.

(Pause. They stare into each other's eyes.)

EVELYN It wasn't the painting, per se. It was the time, the quote, unquote "obsessive amount of time that I was giving to"—that night Darryl—let's just say "clarified" my proper mission as wife, mother. Hostess. It was the row of our . . . Well.

KATE I would've kept on.

EVELYN Pardon me?

KATE On the side, on the sly—whatever. Not to put you down, I know yours was a different generation. But hey— I would've found ways to—

EVELYN *(Moving in on* KATE.*)* Then *why* haven't you? *(*KATE *stops still.)* You see yes. No. No. *(Points to herself.)* Let's put the blame where it belongs. Darryl provided me with the excuse. Truth is, I couldn't stand fretting about being good enough. "Fretting"? Ha! More like tearing my hair out.

KATE *(Softly, understanding)* Yes. *(Pause.)*

EVELYN But see, a lifetime of amateur work is better than living on empty.

KATE My situation's entirely different.

*(*EVELYN *takes her hand.)*

EVELYN Oh? Fine. Be like me—taking down the dusty, dried-up palette after forty years . . . *(Pause.)* Is that what you want?

(A moment, as the two women hold hands. EVELYN, *over in her space, removes her painting apron and packs up the oblong box. Lights simultaneously remain on* LEON *behind the wheel.)*

EVELYN Too bad I'm off to Santa Fe so soon. We could paint together often. Oh, I would have loved that.

KATE I warn you. When I did paint, I always painted butt-naked.

EVELYN Ha. I'm game.

(Pause. KATE *smiles at* EVELYN. *Then drops smile. She turns and addresses* LEON, *who remains in the car.)*

KATE I forgot.

(Pause.)

LEON *(From his side of the stage)* Forgot?

KATE My secret. That I had one.

(Pause.)

LEON *(Softly)* Baby.

EVELYN *(To* KATE*)* Now then, since your mortgage came through with, as they say, "flying colors," let's have the closing by the twenty-fifth, shall we?

KATE *(To* EVELYN*)* Fantastic.

EVELYN Ha. My neighbors won't be surprised that I waited till I found an artist type to replace me. They're all very, very friendly people, by the way. Be sure to introduce yourself around. There's an annual neighborhood Maiden Lake barbecue and boat race every Labor Day. *(Pause. She holds up a set of paintbrushes that are wrapped with a ribbon—a gift to* KATE*—playfully.)* Just don't forget these. These'll keep your life awake. Promise?

KATE *(Offers her hand.)* Thanks again.

EVELYN No need for that. I'm sure it's a great relief to get off Taylor Avenue.

KATE Ha, our house now's so tight.

EVELYN Now you'll have space for your nursery and your studio. You'll never feel cramped on Maiden Lane.

KATE *(Beat.)* Right.

EVELYN And thanks to all your brand-new neighbors, the character of the neighborhood will never "shift." *(Pause.)* If you know what I mean.

KATE *(Pause. Turning to* LEON*.)* Bam. Cold water to the face. Reality check. Three weeks of afternoons being—"them" with her. And—yes—loving it. Them. *(Pause.)* Not to be the Katie who the black girls called "snow white." And not the Katie who the white kids called "weird" whenever I corrected them to say I was black. *(Pause.)* To be just a woman painting. And belonging there. Not weighted down by a secret. *(Pause.)* Almost friends, painting.

*(*EVELYN *studies* KATE*.)*

EVELYN You do—understand me.

(KATE *turns back to* EVELYN.)

KATE *(Brightly)* Oh. Perfectly. Yes. Quite.

EVELYN We Maiden Laners have a pact.

KATE Ah.

EVELYN Protecting the gates. So to speak.

KATE Mmmm. I—uh—agree.

EVELYN "Keeping the lake pristine" is what Wally McCallister says.
Crude perhaps, but he has a point. (KATE *seems to be covering her
face, perhaps hiding tears.*) My dear?

KATE Ah, eyelash in my . . . eye. (EVELYN *starts to rush toward her.
She pulls away, recovering herself.*) Nono. I got it. I'm fine. I'm
fine.

EVELYN As I was saying, you know, just wanted to . . . clarify.

(KATE *nods, with a bright smile on her face.*)

KATE *(To* LEON *and to herself)* Keep nodding . . . keep nodding. *(To*
EVELYN*)* Right.

EVELYN *(Smiling.)* Welcome to Maiden Lane.

(EVELYN *fades into the shadows as she continues to speak.* KATE *crosses
back to* LEON, *sitting beside him in the car.* LEON *holds and
comforts* KATE, *cradles her as she wipes her tears. He kisses her
face.*)

LEON Sh-h-h-h.

KATE *(Ironic)* Mother's term for me would be a "Judas to the race."

LEON Naw-naw, we don't go there, that's b.s. You knew you were
pretending, then you—forgot for a bit, that's all it was.

KATE I dunno, who knows, who cares. Let's never bring it up again.

(LEON *turns and calls out as if* EVELYN *is actually watching, which she is
not.*)

LEON Well, we in there now—bitch! *(To* KATE*)* Hope them bastards do try coming after us. I'll sic a team of legal eagles on they asses quicker than they can spell "grits"— Just try something—just try something! (KATE *starts laughing uncontrollably.*) What? Tell me. Katie, what?

KATE Wait'll they E-mail Evelyn in Santa Fe. *(Calling out to the air)* Hey, Evelyn! I've got all kinds of paint on me, baby!

LEON Let's get you to bed, so I can cover you with kisses. *(Pause as he begins to start the car. Calling out to the air)* Yeah, I hope y'all do try and start up with us, shi-it! I'll get the folks who can get us Jesse Jackson, even fucking Al Sharpton, shit. You'll have such a media circus on Maiden Lane, you'll be *paying* us to stay!

KATE Great. That's all I need.

LEON Huh?

KATE Public media hoopla about how I "passed" to get us into a house. Mother'd be real proud.

LEON Wait—wait—

KATE Spare me the act—okay? It happened to me. Period. There's no need to pretend that you can make it go away.

LEON What the— You the one got us started in this whole mess.

KATE Oh, thank you. Been waiting for that.

LEON It's the truth! Didn't consult me, did you? Decided to go window-shopping by yourself.

KATE *(Mocking)* That's right, all my fault. Let *me* shoulder all the blame.

LEON Naw-naw, I fucking-ass agreed to it, sure. Put my seal of approval on the whole damn—

KATE Yes! Please take some responsibility for your part for once.

LEON *(Pounding his fists.)* Aaaagh!

KATE I put my self-respect on the line for us! For you to have this, too, and then you have the gall to blame me!!

LEON Me turning myself into this "invisible man" crap day after day after . . . day!

KATE Didn't you say "Let's test her. Tell her hello from your husband in—"

LEON Maybe the make-believe me is the guy you *really* want.

KATE Talk sense!

LEON A white guy wouldn't embarrass you, baby!

KATE Don't be ridiculous!

LEON I'll have my stuff out by Friday. Tomorrow I'll call you, let you know where I'm staying.

KATE What!! *What??*

LEON I'll drop you back at the house.

KATE Stop this! Stop it!!

LEON I'm the secret you forgot this afternoon—and wanted to forget!

KATE That— No. That is not true.

LEON You been so tangled up in make believe—how would you know what's true? And how long is this lie supposed to go on in the family, anyway? Huh? To the third, fourth generation?

KATE Don't do this.

LEON Leave it to our grandkids to investigate—find out how we really got—(*He signals toward the house.*)

KATE Lee, let's just calm down.

LEON I really have been "away on business"—that's the kick. *Ha!* Out of sight, out of mind—

KATE Please, please. This is the worst day of my— Please, please—

LEON And it's all still about you, still about you! (*She moves to touch him, he backs away.*) Don't! (*Suddenly there is the sound of a car. Headlights start to stream across their faces.*) Shit. Cops. (*They freeze. The headlights continue, then pass on. A pause. They relax. Sound of a* *car turning around, the headlights return.)* Fuck. They're turning around.

(KATE takes his hand.)

KATE *(Softly)* It's all right, baby. It's all right.

LEON Least I'm still in my fucking suit'n'tie. Fuck.

KATE Not to panic—that's the—that's—not to—not—that's— Don't make a move. Keep smiling. Oh damn, the binoculars!

(We hear a blaring police radio. Headlights shine bright, right into their faces. LEON mimes rolling down a window, smiling stiffly, and waving. A searchlight-like light glares straight into KATE's and LEON's faces.)

LEON *(Smiles, gritting his teeth.)* Fuck fuck fuck.

KATE *(Smiling into the lights.)* Take it easy, darling—easy.

(Unseen POLICEMAN'S VOICE comes over a bullhorn.)

POLICEMAN'S VOICE What's goin on?!

LEON *(Nods to unseen face.)* Just car trouble, Officer, fine now. We're fine!! *(He mimes turning on the ignition; it stalls for one tense second, then comes on.)* Just fine.

(KATE wraps her arm around LEON.)

KATE *(Smiling to unseen face.)* Out for a drive, we got lost. *(Nods again.)*

(LEON nods to the unseen face as KATE smiles. Their eyes follow the headlights as the police car drives away. They drop their smiles. Silence. They turn and stare at each other. Fadeout.)

In the Western Garden

›STUART SPENCER

'99

ORIGINAL PRODUCTION

DIRECTOR Judy Minor
SET DESIGNER Kenichi Toki
COSTUME DESIGNER Amela Baksic
SOUND Beatrice Terry
PROPS Erika Malone
PRODUCTION STAGE MANAGER Gretchen A. Knowlton
STAGE MANAGER Paul Powell

The cast was as follows:
GENE Robert Hogan
LEONARD David Margulies
ALAN Rob Morrow
SALLY Peggity Price

CHARACTERS

GENE KAAP in his sixties

SALLY KAAP in her forties

LEONARD

ALAN

PLACE

Late 1980s, the terrace of a house on the East End of Long Island—"the Hamptons"

TIME

11 a.m. Summer. A beautiful, sun-drenched day

"It is closing time in the gardens of the west, and from now on an artist will be judged only by the resonance of his solitude or the quality of his despair."

—CYRIL CONNOLLY

The Unquiet Grave

A door upstage leading into the house. There are also exits stage left and stage right. Stage left exit goes toward a barn, now serving as an artist's studio. Stage right goes toward the driveway. Several chairs and a table are set out on the terrace.

SALLY *sits in one of the chairs, reading a magazine, sipping a cup of coffee.* GENE *enters from stage left. He carries a basket of tomatoes. He goes to look around the corner to the driveway.*

SALLY He's not here yet.

GENE No, I was just . . . uh . . .

SALLY Enjoying the view?

GENE Yes.

SALLY Pretty driveway, isn't it? Gravel's a nice touch. *(She looks back at her magazine.)*

GENE I don't want him getting the jump on me.

SALLY Three-hour drive this time of year. Traffic and all. I say one o'clock at the earliest.

(Pause.)

GENE How long is he staying?

SALLY He didn't say.

GENE You didn't ask him?

SALLY Don't worry. You know he won't want to spend a night outside the city. He's like a vampire—always home by sunset.

GENE A vampire would be *sunrise*, I think.

SALLY You get the idea.

(Beat. SALLY *reads.* GENE *examines the tomatoes.)*

GENE Good tomatoes this year.

SALLY They're wonderful.

GENE Eat 'em like apples.

SALLY Mmm.

GENE What are you going to tell him?

SALLY What am *I* going to . . . *I'm* not saying anything. This is your business.

GENE But you're so much better at this.

SALLY There's nothing to be good at.

GENE Please? I'll get scarce, you tell him, he'll go away, I'll make tomato soup.

SALLY If you want me to tell him to go away, that I can do. But if anyone is going to give him the news, Gene, that person is you.

GENE I thought that's what I had you for. *(The sound of a car pulling in.)* Oh God.

SALLY If you explain, he'll understand.

(GENE looks around him.)

GENE No, he won't. I've got to hide.

SALLY Don't you dare. He's come all the way from the city.

(Car doors open and slam shut. He pecks her on the forehead.)

GENE Thank you. You've never let me down.

(He exits the way he came, toward the studio. She looks after him, annoyed. She makes a decision, then exits into the house. A young man, ALAN, enters. He stops as though sensing something strange.)

ALAN Damn. It's got a *vibe*.

(LEONARD appears behind him.)

LEONARD What did you say?

ALAN This place, it's got his vibe. I can feel him.

(He has sunk to his knees, putting his cheek on the earth. LEONARD rolls his eyes.)

LEONARD Alan, this is me. You can save the drama.

(ALAN stands up, satisfied—not in response to LEONARD.)

ALAN You could feel it, too, if you weren't so fucking tense. Where do you think he is?

LEONARD Hiding.

ALAN Hiding?

LEONARD Gene likes to hide. It's why he left the city, came here. It was remote at the time. Hard to get to. Suited him perfectly.

(ALAN wanders around, inspecting the details of the place.)

ALAN Well, it's a good pose, anyway.

LEONARD It's not a *pose*. Gene's not the posing type.

ALAN You don't take a place in the Hamptons if it's not some kind of pose.

LEONARD It wasn't "the Hamptons" at the time, it was the East End: potato farmers and fishermen. It was cheap, and the light was good, and nobody bothered him. That's why they all came—Pollock, de Kooning. All of them. Gene's not a *poseur*. He's no good at it.

ALAN That's what makes him good at it: that he's not "good at it."

LEONARD Your problem is you have no perspective.

ALAN *(Stung, angry)* No, Leonard, it's not lack of perspective. It's a different one. My perspective is that I understand perception, and the perception is Gene Kaap lives in the Hamptons. That's what people say. That's how they think of it. They don't think about old potato farms. They think Gene Kaap/Hamptons, Hamptons/Gene Kaap. One does not see him moving to some other potato farm in some other remote area, does one? A pose is a pose, whether it's stumbled upon by accident or deliberately struck. He's associating himself with the place. It's all about marketing, Leonard, raising the value of the work. A subject you'd know something about.

LEONARD Gene's got all the money he can use.

ALAN A man with a lot of money and a major reputation goes to some effort to acquire greater cachet and make even more money. Why? Because he can, Leonard. Back to Art Dealer School with you.

(LEONARD stands.)

LEONARD I shouldn't have brought you.

ALAN I'm only telling the truth and you know it.

LEONARD If you embarrass me in front of him . . .

ALAN Oh, Leonard, relax. Gene and I are going to get along fine.

LEONARD Just don't screw it up. This is too important. I'm going to look for him. *(He goes toward the orchard.)*

ALAN Shouldn't you try the house? *(He points to the house.)*

LEONARD He's not there.

ALAN How do you know?

LEONARD There's one thing you should know about me: I know Gene.

(He leaves. ALAN *watches him go, then drops down to put his face to the ground again.* SALLY *appears at the screen door, and not seeing* ALAN, *she enters. He looks up, she sees him, but it's too late. They look at each other.)*

ALAN You must be Mrs. Kaap.

SALLY And you are?

ALAN Alan.

SALLY *(Lightly, not snide)* What, is that like Cher? You're "Alan"?

ALAN Alan Becker.

SALLY *(A light goes off.)* Wait a second . . . *(She picks up the magazine.)* I was just—Aren't you in here?

ALAN *(Looking at the cover.)* Oh, this is old.

SALLY *(Looking for the article.)* Well, we're a little behind the times around here. Here you are. "Installation Nation: Alan Becker and the Art of Perception."

ALAN I wasn't that happy with it, actually.

SALLY No?

ALAN Not the magazine piece, that was fine. I meant my installation—it never really seemed to work totally.

SALLY You're being modest.

ALAN No, it's true. It was too direct, too—I don't know . . .

SALLY *(Encouraging him to go on)* Yes?

ALAN Too . . . *clear*.

SALLY Right.

ALAN My work has to be more veiled, more stratified. It's got to . . . You can't take it head on. It has to be . . .

SALLY . . . less clear.

ALAN Right.

SALLY Less emotional.

ALAN Well, not without some kind of . . . *slant* anyway.

SALLY Got it.

ALAN I'm doing this new installation downtown at Kinesis—you know it?

SALLY *(Not completely sure)* Kinesis . . .

ALAN It's new. Anyway, my piece is going to be good, I think. I hope. I mean, if things work out . . .

(He wants to say something but can't. She's aware of that and chooses to move on regardless.)

SALLY Where's Leonard?

ALAN He went to look for Gene.

SALLY In the studio?

ALAN *(Looking offstage.)* If that's the studio back there. Leonard seemed to think he was hiding.

SALLY Oh, did he.

ALAN Is he?

SALLY Oh, I can't speak for Gene. That's a long-standing policy. I'm not about to break it. Hungry?

ALAN Uh . . . no. Thanks.

SALLY I hope you like tomatoes. Bumper crop this year. We're having them for lunch.

ALAN Could I ask you something? *(She looks at him, noncommittal.)* Do you think it would be okay if I kind of . . . talked to him? Alone?

SALLY To Gene?

ALAN Yeah.

SALLY About what?

ALAN Well—his work, basically. The old stuff—from the fifties and
sixties.

SALLY I'm afraid they were all bought a very long time ago—

ALAN *Buy* one!? What do you think I am? A millionaire? Jesus, no.
I just want to . . . I'd just love to *talk* to him about them.

SALLY Oh, well, he *loves* to talk . . .

ALAN I mean, not *just* talk. It's about this new project. I got an idea
on the way out here, in the car. I really think it might be kind
of genius.

SALLY What kind of idea?

ALAN I can't tell you.

SALLY Why not?

ALAN It wouldn't be right. It wouldn't come out the right way.

SALLY How would it come out?

ALAN Look, I know you're the gatekeeper . . .

SALLY I beg your pardon.

ALAN Mrs. Kaap, I don't want to dance around. That's what you
are, everybody knows that.

SALLY Well, I hate to be the one to—

ALAN Which I respect. That's why I'm coming to you directly, for
permission. Just to talk to him.

SALLY And you can't say what it's about.

ALAN It's not about sales or contracts or money. That much I guarantee. I guess I just want his blessing for what I want to do.

SALLY I'm sorry, but this is all just too vague . . .

ALAN Okay, look. What I do in my work—it's about perception.
Getting people to look on different levels. When Gene was
starting out, all he had to do was paint.

SALLY Actually he had to paint *well*.

ALAN Of course . . .

SALLY That part was always crucial . . .

ALAN Yes, of course . . .

SALLY But often forgotten.

ALAN I didn't mean that. Of course. You're right. But that's still my point—you could simply be very good. Which is hard enough—but at least there wasn't this whole other level of having to make some sort of splash that has nothing to do with being "very good."

SALLY I don't see why you're complaining.

ALAN It's not a complaint—

SALLY That article seems to say that making a splash is your *forte*.

ALAN It's an observation. I don't complain.

SALLY And this idea of yours, the reason you want to talk to Gene—it's about making that splash.

ALAN It has artistic merit. *(She only stares at him.)* This isn't going to do it justice, because you have to be there and see it to understand. I mean, it would be like explaining one of Gene Kaap's paintings to someone who's never seen one.

SALLY Try me.

ALAN *(Suddenly into it)* Okay, I converted the entire floor of the gallery into a blacktop, like the surface of an old parking lot. Worked into the floor, I have coins, I have matches, I have cigarettes, bottle tops, pop tops, rubber bands, paper clips, condoms, nuts, bolts, screws, old wire, audio tape, gum, candy wrappers. The detritus of a so-called civilization.

So you walk into this gallery and the first thing you notice is that you don't really notice anything. Because there's nothing on the walls. It's all on the floor, and the entire floor is the installation, so you don't see it right away—you don't *recognize* it. You just think, Oh, this building has a really weird floor. And it's SoHo, so you figure, this was a garage or something and nobody ever bothered to fix up the floor.

So you go into the back, where there's an office, and you ask where the installation is, and they say "Out front." And you go back out front and you look again, and then—maybe, if you're smart—you look down and you think, Wait a minute. This is it. This is the installation. Which is when you start to get it.

The exciting moment is when they begin to see, to apprehend the true nature of what they're looking at—the moment of the shift, the revelation of meaning. They're forced to stop looking at it one way and start looking at it another. That's what it's all about. And the problem is, that's not happening. I have to incorporate another level of apprehension.

SALLY Which is where Gene comes in . . .

ALAN Exactly.

SALLY How?

ALAN That's what I can't tell you. I've got to say it to him. It wouldn't feel right otherwise.

SALLY I'm afraid I haven't seen him all morning.

ALAN But he's around . . .

SALLY Sometimes he's gone for hours . . .

ALAN He should be the one to decide—you said so yourself. Otherwise it's really you who's making the decision

(LEONARD *has entered during this.* SALLY *sees him before* ALAN *does and uses it as an escape.*)

SALLY Leonard . . .

(*She rises; they kiss.*)

LEONARD You're looking very well.

SALLY Spoken like an expert in press relations.

LEONARD Whatever he wants, don't trust him.

ALAN Oh, that's nice.

LEONARD Or at least make him pay for it.

ALAN This is my own dealer talking.

SALLY *(To* LEONARD*)* You didn't find him out there?

LEONARD No.

SALLY Well, he does disappear, you know.

LEONARD You don't know where he is?

ALAN She doesn't give up much info, Leonard.

SALLY You know Gene. In the old days he might be gone for *days*.

LEONARD Yes, but that was the old days.

SALLY Some things never change.

LEONARD *(Tiring of this)* Sally, where is he?

SALLY I don't have the foggiest.

(Slight pause.)

LEONARD Alan, there's lots of weird rusted iron . . . *stuff* behind the barn. Why don't you go have a look.

ALAN Leonard, I'm a big boy now.

LEONARD If you find something you want, maybe Sally will let you throw it in the trunk.

ALAN You're so subtle. *(He exits.)*

SALLY We're not going to have a scene now, are we?

LEONARD I hope not.

SALLY How about a tomato? They're really good. We grow them out by the studio. Gene's very proud of them.

LEONARD Sally, stop it.

SALLY I tried to tell you about his health.

LEONARD You said he got tired.

SALLY Yes. He's probably tired.

LEONARD Then he's inside, lying down.

SALLY No, he's—he might have gone for a walk.

LEONARD Well, which is it?

SALLY I don't know.

LEONARD Sally . . .

SALLY I tried to warn you on the phone—

LEONARD . . . if you're interfering somehow—

SALLY —but he was standing there in the room. I couldn't very well spell it all out.

LEONARD Spell what out?

SALLY His mind, Leonard. *(Pause. She struggles.)* It's . . . Well, it's not *gone*, not completely. He'll be right here, perfectly fine. I'll go inside the house to answer the phone, come back out, and . . . he'll be gone. Here, but disappeared into some . . . blank, empty place.

And sometimes . . . he's *gone gone*. He went out to the studio one morning and never came back. I finally had to call the police. He'd gotten lost a hundred yards from the house—ended up in Water Mill. Didn't recognize a thing. Two days later, he woke up the same old Gene again.

LEONARD *(Stunned)* How long has this been going on?

SALLY He started to forget things after we moved out here full-time. For five years he worked every day, though. And even after that, he still went out to the studio, because—well, he always said that painting was like going through a secret door, into another world. And who would stop trying to go through that door—even if he couldn't find it?

LEONARD God, Sally . . . I'm sorry.

SALLY Oh, I'm used to it now. The only hard part is, he'll be gone for good one day. That I won't like.

LEONARD I always thought you were the one good thing he ever had.

SALLY Well, I wouldn't go that far . . .

LEONARD Face it, except for you, who was there?

SALLY *(Smiling ruefully.)* Well, no one else was crazy enough to be in love with him. Then again, I had his work. I always had the feeling Gene was speaking right to me, saying all the things he couldn't say otherwise. *(Her smile evaporates.)* Oh Jesus, I've got to stop that.

LEONARD But it's true . . .

SALLY No—talking in the past tense. There'll be plenty of time for that.

LEONARD You were the only one who never wanted anything of him. That includes me. And nothing much has changed, I'm afraid. *(Pause.)* I'm broke. *(She looks at him as if she didn't hear correctly.)* Out of money.

SALLY That's impossible.

LEONARD I used to think so, too.

SALLY You've got a gallery full of work. *(Referring to the magazine again)* I keep reading about it.

LEONARD Oh, the work is still there. A year ago it was worth three and a half, maybe four million. Today . . . well, today I wish there were a market for scrap canvas.

It's over, Sally. Nobody's had that kind of money since the crash—and what they've got they aren't spending on art. I'm stuck.

SALLY *(With a nod out toward the studio.)* Enfant terrible can't help you out?

LEONARD Are you kidding?

SALLY He seems to be all the rage.

LEONARD Yeah, but it's tough to take an asphalt floor containing "the detritus of our so-called civilization" and hang it over your couch.

I know about the paintings, Sally.

SALLY What paintings?

LEONARD Stop it. I got a call from Misha Kansky and he said Gene had mentioned them.

SALLY I knew it.

LEONARD Sally, these are important paintings. From what you're saying, maybe the last he'll ever do. The world deserves to see them. Gene deserves to show them.

SALLY Leonard, I can't.

LEONARD And you know I'm the person to sell them.

SALLY You would be, of course, if—

LEONARD I'd do it right. Tasteful, but profitable.

SALLY You just said you couldn't sell anything.

LEONARD *(Slight pause. Surprised she needs this explanation)* New work by Gene Kaap . . . that I can sell. It's been fifteen years. Do you know how badly people want to see what he's done in that time? It's one of the great mysteries of the art world. What has Gene Kaap been up to since then?

SALLY Leonard, it's not up to me. You know that. Gene and I have always agreed that the work is his. His to sell, his to keep, his to do with as he pleases.

LEONARD *(With difficulty)* They're going to seize the assets.

SALLY Your paintings?

LEONARD Not just the paintings. The gallery. The apartment. My socks and underwear. Everything.

SALLY Oh my God . . .

LEONARD They'd be gone already, but I was able to convince them I had a shot at this. Thank God, I found a bank officer who had actually heard of him. I kept dropping his name in front of these blank-eyed CPAs . . .

Sally, at least show them to me.

SALLY I'm sorry. You're going to have to talk to Gene. It's the only way.

LEONARD Boy, are you tough.

SALLY I'm not tough, Leonard.

LEONARD You really think you're doing him a favor when you act like this.

SALLY No, I think I don't have a choice. *(She looks at him, feeling bad.)* Let me show you the garden. The tomatoes really are quite good this year. You want to pick a basket?

LEONARD I don't like tomatoes.

SALLY You don't have to eat them. You can just look at them. *(She heads to the studio. He still hesitates.)* Maybe we'll find him out there.

LEONARD *(He takes the basket.)* Lead the way.

(They exit. After a moment, GENE *enters from the house. He looks both ways, then goes to retrieve the tomatoes.* ALAN *enters from the driveway.* GENE *is caught.)*

GENE Shit.

ALAN Hi.

GENE You must be the . . . uh . . . in the magazine . . . *(He nods to the magazine, which happens to be near.)*

ALAN Alan Becker.

GENE Right. Gene Kaap.

ALAN I know.

GENE Where's Leonard?

ALAN I don't know. They were just here. Maybe she's showing him your studio.

GENE Oh yeah?

ALAN We could stop them.

GENE No, I don't give a shit.

ALAN Well, this is an honor. *(He goes to shake* GENE's *hand.* GENE *puts down the tomatoes and they shake.)* For the longest time, I thought you were dead.

GENE Yeah, me too.

ALAN I hope it's okay I'm here. I happened to run into Leonard last night at an opening and—Well, I really had to beg him. Because of your privacy and all.

GENE Nice of him.

ALAN It is kind of perfect, though, isn't it?

GENE Is it?

ALAN That we got the chance to meet.

GENE Why is that perfect?

ALAN Well—one generation to another. Former iconoclast to current iconoclast.

GENE Oh. Right.

ALAN Well, you were. I mean, you are.

GENE That's a lot of bullshit. If I could have been Norman Rockwell, believe me—in a heartbeat.

ALAN *(Genuine)* You know, I respect the hell out of that.

GENE You do?

ALAN You are what you have to be—no complaints. That's exactly why I thought I could—*(He glances out toward the studio to make sure they're alone.)* Listen, I've got this idea. Do you mind if I just pitch it to you? It's crazy but . . . Is that okay?

GENE I don't know. I never got pitched before.

ALAN I've got a show coming up, an installation at Kinesis. And I had this idea, coming out here in the car, that you—your work—I want to use it.

GENE I don't do group shows.

ALAN No, that's not what I—

GENE I always come off looking bad.

ALAN Gene, it's not—

GENE My stuff is fragile—

ALAN —can I call you Gene?

GENE —it doesn't look fragile, but it is.

ALAN It's not a group show. It's an installation. But I want you to be in it—be part of it. Or it to be part of you—whichever way you want to think about it. *(GENE is completely confused.)* You're not getting this.

GENE No . . .

ALAN What I did was, I converted the floor into a blacktop, like the surface of an old parking lot. Then I worked all kinds of . . . *junk* basically—the detritus . . .

GENE . . . of a so-called civilization.

ALAN *(How did he know that?)* Right . . .

GENE I was listening at the window.

ALAN *(Barely a pause to regroup.)* So you—okay. But what I didn't say is . . . the idea was—originally—that the walls were bare, so that you came into the gallery and saw bare walls and thought, What's this? Bare walls. Nothing here. And then slowly, *eventually*, you caught on to the floor.

But in the car, on the way out here, I got to thinking, Well, here I am, meeting Gene Kaap. That's got to mean something. What does it mean?

GENE And what did it mean?

ALAN What if we take posters—not the actual paintings—but *posters* of your work from the mid-sixties . . . you know, *Inversion #5* or *Black on Red*—and we hang them on the wall, so they're sort of like *looking down on* this . . . this *trash*, really. This remnant of culture. I mean, that just sounds so exciting—and for you, such a great way for people to see your work again. To see it new, fresh.

GENE Who the fuck *are* you?

ALAN Look, I'm sort of excited. I'm not explaining it very well. But it's a way to bridge the gap, you see?

GENE What *gap*?

ALAN Between you and me, the past and present, your world and this one.

GENE This is bullshit.

ALAN Look, what I do . . . it's different than what you did. You haven't been around.

GENE Yeah, and I'm starting to feel grateful.

ALAN This is a tribute. It's an homage.

GENE I hate tributes.

ALAN Well, you could use one, frankly. People don't care anymore, Gene. People aren't talking about you.

GENE I don't want them to talk about *me*.

ALAN Or the work.

GENE This year, they're bored. Next year, a retrospective and I'm rediscovered.

ALAN Yes, exactly.

GENE For that I don't need your help.

ALAN I hate to say it, but you do.

GENE Stuck up on a poster? A decoration on the wall?

ALAN Because it won't just be your work. It'll be a comment on my work.

GENE Nobody's putting up any posters of anything of mine, anywhere.

ALAN Well, I don't exactly need your permission. The posters exist.

GENE Not for that purpose.

ALAN No. For advertising. And that's okay, I suppose. And for sale in the museum shops. And that's okay, too. You're happy to stoop when it comes to merchandising. *(He realizes this is only making it worse.)* Look, I admire and respect you. And your work.

GENE Forgive me if I'm not flattered. People see my work every day, all over the world, and so far they haven't needed you to help them. Go ask Pollock or Newman or Rothko if they want to be in your installation. They're all dead. They can't say no.

ALAN Oh, you can't say no either.

GENE I just did.

ALAN Anybody can buy a poster of your work and hang it on a wall and say, "This is a poster of Gene Kaap's *Black on Red*." There's no copyright law against that.

GENE I'll sue.

ALAN Good. I could use the publicity. Especially when you lose.

GENE Listen, you pipsqueak. I made something. That makes it mine. You can't have it.

ALAN Oh, come on. Did you really "make something"? You put paint on canvas, yes. But you were only translating. "Create" is this word some egomaniac came up with to convince himself that what he was doing was important. And art *was* important. But now we've done it. We've been there. There is no such thing as creativity. Only arrangement. And I'm not afraid to say it.

GENE When I painted the world the way *I* painted the world, no-body had ever done that before. I created the emotions, in here . . . *(His torso)* and I created the means by which to express them. That paint and those feelings together—that was some-thing new.

ALAN You're really letting this get way too emotional.

GENE Right! Because you wouldn't know an emotion if it crawled up your asshole and built a nest there.

(This is stinging—it's enough for ALAN.*)*

ALAN You know, I'd heard you were arrogant, but . . .

GENE You heard right . . .

ALAN But a philistine—that I never . . .

GENE . . . because I draw the line somewhere!

ALAN *(Lashing out)* Because you can't imagine anyone taking what you did and going the next step. No, the work has to stop with you. You're the pinnacle.

GENE I never said that.

ALAN But you don't have to, do you?

GENE Go further—yes, but the only way you're going is— Well, all this relentless *irony*, this intellectualism, the cool surface, the godawful commentary. Where's the humanity?!

ALAN *(Angry and hurt)* I am responding to the world as it is. As I see it, as I *understand* it. It's different now, Gene. Come down off Mount Olympus . . . We're struggling down here! You think I wouldn't like it the way it was? You think I'm not jealous of the way you lived and worked? *(Resolved now, sure of himself)* But that's over. People laugh at emotion now. *I* laugh at it. And I hate that about the world, but there it is. That's the way it is *now*. What am I supposed to do? Ignore that? I can't make the world a different place, and I can't lie about it either. If it's one thing I won't do, it's lie. Ironic? Yes, guilty—fine. But that's the truth about the world I see. *(Wondering if he went too far)* I love your work, Gene. I honor it. All I'm asking is, let me pay you that honor.

GENE You're a goddamned thief!

(LEONARD and SALLY have entered on this last line. They have a basket of tomatoes.)

LEONARD You've obviously met.

SALLY *(Worried)* Gene . . .

GENE Keep your goddamned hands off my work!

(He sits down. SALLY goes to him.)

LEONARD I'm sorry—whatever he said . . .

ALAN Hey, I'm not some *criminal*.

LEONARD We have yet to determine that.

ALAN I'm allowed to have a point of view.

LEONARD No, you're not. *(He looks to* SALLY, *who has gone to* GENE.*)*

SALLY Are you all right?

GENE I'm fine.

SALLY Your breathing is off.

GENE Oh, for Christ's sake, I'm all right. Blew the damn carbon out of my pistons, that's all!

SALLY *(To* LEONARD*)* He gets like this. I can't do a thing.

LEONARD What do you mean, "gets"? He's been like this his whole life, Sally.

GENE How the hell are you, Len? Get over here. *(*LEONARD *goes to him.* GENE *grabs him in a bear hug, then looks at him.)* You prick. What are you trying to do, bringing this little twit with you?— give me a stroke?

LEONARD Gene, I'm sorry if he—whatever he said. He's got a mouth . . .

ALAN Hey, knock off the apologies!

SALLY Gene, you're going to overdo it.

GENE Good. Let's overdo it. Pipsqueak here got me on a roll.

LEONARD He's full of himself, okay—but he's also talented.

GENE Oh, gimme a break . . .

LEONARD You've never even seen his work.

GENE I saw that article. *(He indicates the magazine.)*

ALAN And I suppose you'd want people to judge your work based on a magazine spread.

SALLY Look, he's had enough for one day.

GENE You stay out of this.

SALLY Fine—you boys have your fun. I'm out of it. *(She turns and goes to the house. To* ALAN*)* You, with me.

ALAN You can't talk to me like—

SALLY Now.

(She opens the door for ALAN. *He has met his match. He lurches angrily into the house. She follows and lets the door slam.)*

LEONARD Gene, I'm sorry—what can I say?

GENE *(Dismissing it)* You like his stuff. That's your business.

LEONARD You're angry at me.

GENE Lennie, it's your business.

LEONARD He's very good.

GENE All right—so be it.

LEONARD It's not what you do. It's environmental. It's experiential. He's got this whole theory about levels of perception and sequential apprehension, and frankly it's pretty goddamn brilliant. I think he's going someplace very brave, very daring.

GENE Sequential appre— Jesus! Nobody even speaks the same language anymore. We're all just talking up our own assholes.

LEONARD But if we don't go there with him, we're cowards. We're safe. Since when is art safe?

GENE If we go there, the word "art" ceases to have any meaning. You see? It's impossible. We can't even talk about it. Let's talk about the tomato crop.

LEONARD Because you're trying to make a comparison.

GENE I'd just like to know what the kid *does*.

LEONARD You've been asking me that for thirty years. You said the same thing about Roy Lichtenstein. "What the hell does that goddamn kid *do*?"

GENE And I never got an answer *then* either.

LEONARD But it's beneath you—

GENE My ass is beneath me.

LEONARD You don't understand him. Okay. But some people don't understand you either.

GENE But they understand what I did.

LEONARD Not everyone—

GENE If it was any good—and a lot of it wasn't, I'm the first to admit—but if it was any good at all, it was honest to God *me*. My horror, my wonder. My confusion. My love. It was always me. If it wasn't me, I threw it out.

LEONARD And there was never anything like it. Before or since.

GENE You're goddamn right.

LEONARD Which is why I'm here. *(Pause.)* I talked to Misha Kansky.

GENE *(Ready as he'll ever be)* So?

LEONARD He was out here last week. You talked to him. *(A slight beat.)* Gene, I want to see them.

GENE It's impossible.

LEONARD I'm in a bad spot here, I—

GENE I know. I heard. That's my bedroom, right there. *(He indicates the house.)*

LEONARD I'm the right one for your work. I understand it, I know how to handle it.

(GENE has picked up a tomato and is examining it.)

GENE Oh yeah, I know that. *(The tomato)* Beautiful, isn't it? The soil is just right out there behind the barn. You can almost taste the color. If I were a still-life kind of guy, I might try to put it on canvas.

LEONARD Did you?

GENE *(Smiles ruefully.)* I'm not a still-life kind of guy.

LEONARD Gene, I'm asking you. Please. I only want to look at them.

GENE Oh, come on . . .

LEONARD It's up to you whether you want to put them on the market. I'm not going to pressure you. All right, maybe just a little . . .

GENE It wasn't a good time. I wasn't working well.

LEONARD Why don't you let me be the judge of that?

GENE Because you're not as sharp as you used to be, frankly.

LEONARD So you don't trust me—is that it? Because of this kid?

GENE Lennie, the work was not very good. Period.

LEONARD And what if you're being too hard on yourself?

GENE I can't let you see them.

LEONARD So you're just turning your back on thirty years. On us.

GENE I can't show you something that doesn't exist.

LEONARD You had five good years.

GENE I had five years. Nobody said they were good.

LEONARD But you must have something!

GENE I'd have a few good hours, maybe even a day or two at a time. But that's not enough for me. You know the way I work. A day or two? That's nothing! It takes me months—years even.

Every time I went back to the canvas, it was like starting over. So everything got very simple, very plain, but I kept going. I toughed it out, by God. Trying to draw it out, trying to find the heart of it. And one day I looked back at the work I'd done and it looked like a child had been playing with my brushes. Scrawls, Lennie. Kid stuff. And I thought, Oh God, that's not me. It's some *child*—some person I never was, some *other*. It was the one thing I couldn't live with.

So we built a bonfire, Sally and I. Out in back of the studio. Built a nice big pyre, lit it, and waited until the flames were shooting up, licking at the night sky, and then we took every canvas, forty-two of them, and we threw them into the fire, and we watched them turn to vapor. In the morning, nothing but a pile of ashes. Turned out to be good fertilizer. Good for tomatoes. (*He holds up the tomato.*)

LEONARD All of them?

GENE It felt so right, Len.

LEONARD They're all gone?

GENE I didn't know how to tell you. I was chickenshit.

(ALAN *enters from the house.*)

ALAN Leonard, listen, I'm going to take the train back.

LEONARD No, you don't have to—

ALAN I didn't come out here to peel tomatoes, okay? I can catch the 1:05.

LEONARD No, we're going. We're done.

(SALLY *has entered.*)

SALLY You can't go. I'm making lunch.

LEONARD I'm sorry.

ALAN Right now?

LEONARD Yes.

ALAN Give me one minute . . . (*He exits to the studio.*)

SALLY Now you haven't been *fighting*, have you, because—

GENE I told him.

SALLY Oh.

GENE Len, I disappointed you.

LEONARD Yes. And also no, in a funny way.

GENE I did the right thing. I know I did.

(LEONARD *goes to him, takes his right hand into his left.*)

LEONARD Yeah.

GENE You'll get through this with the bank. I'm not worried about you.

LEONARD Goodbye, Gene. I can't stay, I hope you understand.

GENE Drive safe.

(LEONARD *crosses toward the driveway.* SALLY *follows.*)

SALLY (*So that* GENE *doesn't hear.*) I begged him not to, Len.

LEONARD You . . . ?

SALLY I told him, let me save a few. *One*, even. They were gorgeous.

Like Matisse at the very end, the way he blossomed into the
cutouts . . . so simple and so glorious at the same time. That's
what these were.

LEONARD Oh God, don't do this to me . . .

SALLY No—it's better you know. They were beautiful . . . better
that than you believing they were nothing at all.

LEONARD Goodbye, Sally.

SALLY Goodbye.

(ALAN *enters from the studio with a rusted iron thing.* LEONARD *exits to
the driveway.* ALAN *takes one furtive shot at* GENE.)

ALAN Think about it. You deserve it.

(GENE *stares blankly at him, but* ALAN *doesn't see that. He hurries away
under* SALLY's *glare. She watches him go. We hear the car start, doors slam.
As the car drives away, she turns back to* GENE.)

SALLY Well. Glad that's over.

GENE (*Questioningly*) I'm sorry . . .

SALLY Oh, don't worry about it. I knew you'd come through when
you had to.

GENE I don't remember your name.

(*A slight moment.*)

SALLY Sally.

GENE Sally. Sally Sally Sally.

SALLY And you're Gene.

GENE I know.

SALLY Are you hungry?

GENE Yes. Yes, I am.

SALLY I can make lunch for you. Would you like that?

GENE Yes.

SALLY How about a sandwich, with tomatoes?

GENE Tomatoes?

SALLY Right here. Tomato.

GENE Oh . . .

SALLY You like tomatoes.

GENE Yes?

SALLY Oh yes. You like them very much. Go ahead. Try one.

(She hands him a slice. He bites into it. He likes it.)

GENE Mmm. That's good.

SALLY You see? You want me to make a sandwich with tomatoes?
(He nods, his mouth full.) You go ahead and eat the rest of this.
There's lots more. We've got a lot of tomatoes. *(She goes to the
door.)* Don't go away.

*(He nods his head no. She kisses him on the forehead and exits into the
house. He eats as the lights go down.)*

All About Al

'**99**

›CHERIE VOGELSTEIN

ORIGINAL PRODUCTION

DIRECTOR Jamie Richards
SET DESIGNER Kris Stone
COSTUME DESIGNER Amela Baksic
SOUND Beatrice Terry
PROPS Erika Malone
PRODUCTION STAGE MANAGER Gretchen A. Knowlton
STAGE MANAGER Rachel Putnam

The cast was as follows:
GIL Mark Giordano
LENNY Mark Feuerstein
AL Jennifer Carta
COFFEE BAR CUSTOMER JC Cassano

CHARACTERS

GIL

LENNY

AL

COFFEE BAR CUSTOMER

PLACE

A coffee bar in Manhattan on a rainy afternoon

GIL, *very handsome and cool, sits with his back to us in an empty coffee shop, reads the sports section.* LENNY, *downtrodden and uncool, enters in raincoat and galoshes, furtively looks around, spots* GIL, *quickly looks away, orders coffee. Nonchalantly,* LENNY *takes cup and saunters by* GIL's *table. Suddenly he stops, pretends to notice* GIL *for the first time.*

LENNY Gil! *(Practically spills cup.)*

GIL *(Looks up.)* Hey . . . Lenny.

LENNY What a surprise, what a coincidence!

GIL Ye-hah—how ya doin', buddy?

LENNY How are *you*? You look great!

GIL Yeah? Well, I'm doin' okay, you know, hangin' in there. *(Awkward pause, then with some concern)* How uh . . . how are *you* doin', Len?

LENNY *(Jovially)* Me? Well, I'm fine . . . all right, you know . . . not so good. *(Totally serious)* Suicidal—I'm suicidal, Gil.

GIL *(Sympathetic)* Yeah, heard about you and Cindy. I'm sorry, man, we shoulda called.

LENNY No, no, *I* should've called you guys . . . It's just, I've been so preoccupied, you know, with death, I haven't had any time. *(Cheery)* So how's Allison?

GIL Allison? She's real good . . . Yeah, she should be comin' here—

LENNY *(Excited)* Really?!

GIL Yeah.

LENNY Here? Really? *(GIL nods.)* That's great, that is so great!

GIL *(Puzzled by* LENNY's *enthusiasm)* Yeah . . . any minute.

LENNY *(Elated)* I—I can't wait to see her. I mean, what good luck . . . That is so fantastic, just terrific . . . incredible really.

GIL *(Beat.)* You're not gettin' out much, are ya, Len?

LENNY *(Instantly sad. Sits, cradles his head.)* It's hopeless, Gil. I'm miserable. A *wreck*: all alone during allergy season with my hair falling out and my gums big and bleeding— May I join you?

GIL *(Looks around uncomfortably.)* Uh—

LENNY I mean, you don't know how lucky you are—wow—to have a woman like Allison, kind, darling, beautiful Al—

GIL Len—

LENNY *(Raptured)* Oh God, God, I love her like a—*(Realizes)*—a relative, a sister. *(Has to be honest)* A stepsister.

GIL Yeah, I know.

LENNY But she's the last of her species, there are no Allisons left in this world. I thought Cindy might be an Allison, but she, too, turned into a Tina and I—*(He farts, looks up at* GIL *in shocked horror.)* Oh, that is just inexcusable, Gil, I don't know what to say—

GIL It's all right. Lenny, listen—

(They speak at the same time.)

LENNY Ever since Cindy left, my gastrointestinal tract—

GIL —I have to tell ya somethin'—

LENNY —it has a mind of its own . . . I oughta kill myself—

GIL —When Allison gets here—

LENNY —and I will—unless I find a woman.

GIL —I think we're breakin' up.

LENNY *(Shocked)* What?

GIL *(Beat.)* Yeah.

LENNY *(Devastated. Beat.)* No.

GIL *(Beat.)* Yeah . . .

LENNY *(Beat.)* No.

GIL Yeah.

LENNY *(Two beats.)* No.

GIL *(Annoyed)* Lenny.

LENNY I'm sorry, but I . . . can't believe it. I mean, I just can't be-
lieve it—you and Allison, Allison and you . . . you're like
Romeo and Juliet . . . Antony and Cleopatra . . . Laurence
Olivier and Danny Kaye—

GIL *(With distaste)* Oh man . . .

LENNY I'm just so shocked—I'm in shock—wow—*(Shakes his head.
Louder)* Wow. *(Loud. Smiling.)* Wowza!

GIL Well, listen . . . I'm just tellin' ya cuz maybe, you know, it's
not such a good idea for you to be around when I tell her.

LENNY Why, Gil? I'll be very quiet.

GIL Right, but . . . uh . . . even though it's a café deal and I'm
hopin' she'll keep the cryin' violent shit down to a minimum . . .
I'll tell ya, Len, things might get pretty wacky— I mean, it's
not easy breakin' a girl's heart . . . ya know?

LENNY No . . . I don't know. I've dreamt about it . . .

GIL Yeah, well, so anyway . . . I think that's what I'm gonna do.
(He's done with the conversation now.)

LENNY But can you just tell me, Gil, why? I mean . . . why? *(Beat.)*
Why?

GIL What're ya askin' me?

LENNY Well . . . uh . . . *(Beat. A tad perplexed)* I guess I'm asking you why.

GIL But now see, how can I answer somethin' like that? I mean, there're about four million reasons, and no reasons at all except some voice inside ya says it's gotta be done and you can't track down why. It's from a place of no logic, it's not about logic, it's bigger than logic. It's bigger than you. So you listen. *(Beat.)* Cuz once you stop listenin', once you stop, Lenny . . . you're lost. You got no voices left.

LENNY *(Beat.)* Are you shtupping someone else?

GIL *(Immediate)* Yeah.

LENNY *(Horrified)* Are you really?

GIL *(Laughs.)* Hey, gimmee a break, will ya? It's nothin' like that—

LENNY So then what is it, Gil? Really. I want to know. I mean, I *really need* to know! Everybody says they're looking for love, looking for love, looking for love, and what do they do the minute they get it? They flush it away—flush, flush, flush! *(Furious)* This world is just one vast toilet of devotion, one big bathroom of romance where it's better coming out than it was going in. I'm sick of it, I tell you, *sick!* So listen to *this* voice, Gil, and listen good: You're not breaking up with Allison unless you have a damn good reason for it, a damn good reason! Do you hear me, Gil? Do you hear me? *(Yells) Do you hear me?*

GIL *(Beat.)* Are you . . . are you on some kind of medication, Leonard?

LENNY Sinutab— I'm sorry, I'm sorry, but . . . *(Upset again) You're* my friend, too. *(Rises again.)* I won't let you throw your life away! Sure, sure, I may know Allison longer, but let's face it, Gil, we're men—at least you are—and men have to look out for each other: care, bond, love— All right, not love, love's too much, but—

GIL *(Sincerely)* Listen, I appreciate your concern, but . . . uh . . . you got your own problems there, buddy—

LENNY Please, I can always take on more—I welcome it! Gil, don't deprive me of a vicarious thrill. Gil, it's all I have left. *(GIL is weakening.)* If I can help you two work it through, if we can talk it out—

GIL Well, ya know, maybe that's not such a bad idea, cuz like, she's probly gonna ask me why, too, right? So maybe I oughta prepare what I'm gonna say.

LENNY Yes, yes, you definitely should— Wait. *(He turns away, ties a napkin under his chin like a kerchief, turns to face GIL, speaks in falsetto.)* Now— Hi, Gil, how are you?

(GIL looks perplexed.)

GIL What're you doin'?

LENNY *(In falsetto)* I'm Allison—

GIL Oh! *(Laughs.)* No offense, Len, but you make a real ugly girl.

LENNY *(Sticking to his role, falsetto)* Did you want to speak to me about something?

GIL Okay, okay, yeah. *(Seriously)* I did . . . Listen, Al, I have ta tell you something—

LENNY *(Coquettishly)* I love you, Gilly—

GIL Yeah, I love you, too. It's over. We have to break up.

LENNY What?! Why?!

GIL Why? *(Thinks.)* Honestly? Because . . . I have a brain tumor.

LENNY *(Falsetto)* Oh my God! You do?

GIL No, no, no. Seriously? We have to break up because . . . I'm not good enough for you, Al, I think you deserve better.

LENNY *(Falsetto)* I do, but I don't want better, I want you. *(Almost to himself)* —you. Moronic, greasy—

GIL *(Oblivious)* Yeah, but the thing is . . . I don't think I can measure up to this . . . this *image* you have a . . . me, ya know? I

mean, sure we might be good today, we might be good tomorrow, but ultimately I don't have what it takes to fulfill a woman
like you. And one day, one day I'm gonna look into your eyes
and I'm gonna see—instead a the love. I'm gonna see somethin'
else. I'm gonna see all the respect drained out and gone, with
only the hate left. And that's gonna break my heart, Al. *(Sobs.)*
It's gonna fuckin' break my goddamn heart.

LENNY *(As himself)* Wow. Is that true?

GIL No, but it sounded good, right? *(Beat.)* I mean, you can't tell
her the real shit, like . . . like how you hate what she does in
bed!

LENNY What does she do in bed?

GIL Oh well, nothin', nothin', just . . . ya know . . .

LENNY No, I don't know. *(Casually)* I'm willing to know. I
mean . . . I'd *pay* to know—

GIL Well, it's no big deal really, just this thing she does sometimes
when . . . when we're lyin' there . . . ya know, after sex . . . and
I'll be gettin' all comfortable, I'll be startin' to doze off cuz like
. . . I'm *finished*, right?—and all of a sudden, outta nowhere, I'll
feel this leg swingin' over on top of me, right over my body
while I'm tryin' to sleep—

LENNY Is it *her* leg?

GIL Of course it's her leg, that's not the point—the point is, while
I'm tryin' to sleep I don't need some weight pinnin' me down to
the mattress, you know what I mean?

LENNY Cindy bought a bunk bed when I moved in—

GIL I mean, I'm not sayin' I don't appreciate Al's affection. I'm not
saying that at all—but there's a time and a place, and after sex
. . . I do *not* like to be touched, ya know?

LENNY Cindy said even during, it should be kept to a minimum.

GIL Yeah, well, Cindy was a pig—

LENNY *(Defiantly)* But she was my pig.

GIL Listen, Len, can I just say?—she did you the biggest favor in the world when she dumped you.

LENNY I know, I know. That's the one favor women always want to do for me. *(With sudden emotion)* Which is why I'm telling you it's lonely out there, Gil. Allison is special—

GIL Yeah, I know she's special, but . . . but . . . It's not just the leg thing, Lenny. It's more than that . . .

LENNY You mean like a leg/arm kind of thing?

GIL I mean like . . . like—*(Thinks of something.)*—like the way she's so obsessed with her weight! I mean, all she ever does is ask me about it all the time. Like I won't have seen her for a *day* and I'll pick her up and first thing when she opens the door, she'll say, "Hi, Gil, do I look like I gained weight?"

LENNY So?

GIL So I'll say, No, Al, you look great, and she'll say, Are you sure? and I'll say, Positive, and she'll say, No, you're lying, and I'll say, Why would I lie? To make me feel good. No, no way. Yes, I see it in your eyes. No, that's my contact lens, Al. Ya haven't gained an ounce since the day you were born. You promise? I swear. You'd tell me if I did? Of course. You promise you would tell me? I promise. You promise, you promise. I promise, I swear, I swear on my fucking life. Now give me a goddamn stake to put through my head cuz I can't take it anymore, Lenny, it drives me fuckin' nuts!

LENNY Why? *(GIL rolls his eyes in frustration.)* You mean because she's a little insecure about her figure . . . needs a little reassurance, a little positive assessment of her weight?

GIL Yeah, but like . . . why doesn't she just invest inna fuckin' *scale?* ya know what I mean? Why's it have ta be such a big fuckin' *mystery* all the time?

LENNY Gil, Gil, *you're* her scale, Gil, *you.*

(Figure in slicker enters, sits hunched in corner.)

GIL But that's the thing—to me she looks great—so what's she so worried about?

LENNY *(Shrugging.)* Maybe she's afraid if she got fat, you'd break up with her.

GIL *(Softens.)* Well, yeah . . . I would, but that doesn't mean she has to like "dwell," ya know? *(Guiltily)* I mean, come on, Len, every guy wants his girlfriend to have a nice body, right?

LENNY *(Nodding.)* Cindy gained sixty pounds while we were to-gether.

GIL God, I know. *(Eats.)* How'd you deal with that, man?

LENNY I loved her for what was inside.

GIL *(Eating.)* Deep, deep inside—

LENNY *(Impassioned)* Look, a good woman is hard to find.

GIL *(Eating.)* *Cindy's* not hard to find. *(Spreads his arms wide.)*

LENNY Allison's not only beautiful inside *and* out, but she also—

GIL Swallows.

LENNY P-pardon?

GIL Yeah, but ya know, don't mention it, like when she comes.

LENNY Listen, it's not an easy thing to weave into a conversation.

GIL *(Thoughtfully)* The truth is, I don't really give her enough credit for bein' so . . . ya know . . . giving. I mean, she's like a real tribute to her race—ahh, I shouldn't talk about this stuff, it's private shit.

(Beat.)

LENNY Gil, I understand if you don't care to share this topic with me, but let me just say, I'd give my life to hear about it.

GIL *(Hesitates.)* Well . . . all right, just between the two of us. *(Launches ahead.)* What they say about Jewish girls is usually true, right?

LENNY Wha—what do they say about Jewish girls?

GIL Ya know . . . that they're not too big on givin' head—

LENNY Oh. I thought that was all girls.

GIL Yeah, well, I'm just sayin', especially Jewish girls so like, to find a Jewish girl who not only enjoys goin' down but is also willing to . . . imbibe—you're talkin' a rarity. *(LENNY clears his throat, chokes a little.)* Not to be, ya know, too crude—

LENNY *(Quickly)* That's all right, that's fine—

GIL —but Al goes at it like a thirsty sailor on the hot Russian steppe and doesn't come up for air, ya know what I'm sayin'? Don't mention it, Len. Len?

LENNY *(Nodding, choking, takes out inhaler.)* I'm just . . . I'm just having a little difficulty breathing. *(He uses inhaler.)*

GIL *(Looks around, then at his watch.)* I wonder why Al's so late.

LENNY Cindy was always late. Cindy—

GIL Cindy, Cindy, will you forget fuckin' Cindy!

LENNY It just ended last week, Gil.

GIL Yeah, well, get over it already, all right? Get over it!

LENNY *(Repeats to himself)* Get over it.

GIL I mean, the girl treated you like total shit!

LENNY A little worse. *(Figure in slicker cries. They turn briefly.)*

GIL Exactly! So just move on, ya know? move on. You're free!

LENNY Free.

GIL Yeah, yeah—it's a guy's world, Len. I mean, a sixty-year-old man can get a twenty-year-old girl *(He snaps his fingers.)*—like that!

LENNY Really? *(He snaps his fingers.)* Like that?

GIL Nothin' to it.

LENNY So that's it, that's my problem? I'm too young?!

GIL No, no, you're too nice! You like these girls who walk all over ya—

LENNY I do, I'm grateful to them.

GIL —when what you need is somebody nice, somebody sweet, a girl who gives ya support, makes ya feel good, really *likes* you.

LENNY *(Like a kid at a toy store)* They have that?

GIL Yeah, yeah, ya just gotta give yourself a break, buddy, ya know what I mean? Ya gotta . . . go for it, ya know? *(Beat.)* Just go for it!

(Pause.)

LENNY Gil?

GIL Yeah, Len?

LENNY When . . . uh . . . when Allison gets here . . .

GIL Yeah?

LENNY When Allison gets here . . .

GIL Yes?

LENNY When Allison gets here, could I . . . could I . . .

GIL *(Very calm)* Finish the fuckin' sentence, Len.

LENNY . . . have her?

GIL What?

LENNY Well, not "have her." "Have her" is a silly expression, but you know what I mean. Could I ask her out? Would you mind?

GIL *(Incredulous. Then, feigning nonchalance)* Would I mind? If you asked Allison out?

LENNY Yes cuz you said—

GIL You want to ask Allison out?

LENNY Well . . . yes.

GIL *(Beat.)* *My* Allison, right? You mean Allison Kramer.

LENNY Listen, if it's a problem—

GIL No, it's no problem.

LENNY —then I won't—

GIL It's no problem just—

LENNY Just what?

GIL Just nothin', nothin' . . . It's fine.

LENNY Are you sure? Because—

GIL Lenny. I said it's not a problem, okay?

LENNY Okay. *(Beat. Smiling broadly, happily.)* Thanks, Gilly.

GIL Don't call me Gilly, all right? *(Beat. Scowling.)* But I'm just thinkin' . . .

LENNY *(Seriously)* Uh-huh, good, okay—

GIL Ya know . . . what about Cindy?

LENNY Oh. Well, you said to forget her.

GIL And that's it? That's all it takes—I say forget her and you're done?

LENNY Well, Gil, I thought you gave me some very excellent advice, and so I'm trying to follow up on it, is all—

GIL Yeah, well, okay . . . good. *(Takes out cigarette, thinks awhile.)* But I haveta tell ya, Len, maybe this is sick a me an' all, but it kinda does bother me, ya know?

LENNY *(Holds up coffee cup, happy and oblivious.)* This is not decaf.

GIL *(Annoyed)* I mean, you askin' Allison out! I mean, cuz like . . . here you are, and . . . and . . . like . . . the body's still warm, ya know what I'm sayin'?

LENNY Yes, but in a way, isn't that better? *(Smiles broadly.)* I mean, that way she won't have time to mourn over the loss of you because I'll be right there to console her.

GIL *(Getting angrier)* Yeah, but what I'm sayin' is, I don't really want you there to console her.

LENNY But . . . why, Gil? I mean, do you want to see her suffer?

GIL Not at all. But I even more don't want to see her with you.

LENNY But that's not very fair, is it? I mean, here you don't want her anymore—

GIL I never said I didn't *want* her, Lenny.

LENNY Well, you said you were breaking up.

GIL I said I was thinkin' of breaking up—that the little dancin' thought had walked my mind! But I mean I didn't realize that automatically gave *you* the green fuckin' light to pounce?

LENNY *(Frantically looks toward door.)* But you said—

GIL I said a lotta things—because you asked me—as a *friend*— what I was thinkin', so I— wait! Wait. Is that what this whole gig has been about, Lenny, huh?

LENNY Gig? What gig? Please, Gil, I'm gigless.

GIL *(Rises; angrily)* All your concern for the what, why, why— Were you just, ya know, circlin' the area till you could swoop down—like some little galosh-wearin' vulture—

LENNY *(Backing away.)* That's not a very flattering characterization, Gil.

GIL —and . . . and what? just feast on my leftovers?!

LENNY I'm kosher, Gil, please—

GIL I mean, God! you are somethin', man—you are really somethin'—

LENNY How can you say that? You know I'm not something.

GIL —and . . . and I mean for Allison, no less—Allison of all girls. Don't you know how outta your league Allison is?

LENNY Yes of course, but—but you said to go for it!

GIL It. *It*. Not *her*, you asshole!

LENNY *(Summoning up his courage)* But why not? *(Rises.)* Why not her?

GIL Because . . . because . . .

LENNY *(Hitting his stride)* Because what, Gil, *huh*?! All my life I've watched the Leonards of this world lose the Allisons of this world to the Gils of this world, and the Gils don't even care! They don't even fucking care!!! *(He throws* GIL's *saucer against the wall.)*

GIL That's my coffee—

LENNY *(Overlapping)* It's men like you who destroy women for the rest of us—abusing and demeaning and rejecting them till they so totally lose their sense of selves they actually believe the *real* men are the men who treat them that way!

GIL *(Shrugs.)* Yeah, well . . .

LENNY When, in fact, you're not real at all, you're just scared, scared of growing up, scared of yourself, scared that—just like you said in that speech—that one day you're gonna look into her eyes and see the hate, because deep down you believe once Allison sees you, once she really sees Gilly for who he is, she'll see *there's nothing to see!*

GIL Yeah? *(Rises.)* Well— *(Trying to find the right words)*—fuck you, Lenny! Fuck you! *(Screams, grabs* LENNY's *collar.) Fuck you! (Silence. He lets go.)*

LENNY *(Beat.)* I think I've offended you, Gil. *(Sits.)* I'm sorry.

GIL No, don't be sorry, don't be sorry—who wants your sorry, Lenny? I mean, you think I think Al's just some lay . . . some . . . some pop? Well, you're wrong! Allison's a *gift*, a *prize*—who loves me! And so that's a *very* scary thing. *(*LENNY *covers his face.)* I mean, it's a lotta pressure—a lotta— Who wants to deal with disappointin' a girl like that, ya know?! We're not talkin' some bitch whale beast like Cindy— we're talkin' Allison Kramer! And so even if a part a that—if part a what you said—fear—whatever you said—even if it's something involved with that, so what? I mean, what does that prove? That I'm no good, I'm shit? Because I'm—I'm human? That I may be scared of rejection deep down? All right! So what, ya know? Deep down everybody's scared of rejection! Everybody!

LENNY *(Puffing up his chest.)* I'm not!

GIL Well, that's just cuz you're so fuckin' used to it.

LENNY Damn straight! Damn straight I am! *(Rises, speaks quietly.)* Take a look at a real man, Gil—a man who's not afraid of rejection, of intimacy, of commitment, the dark. Well, okay, I am a little afraid of the dark—but I'm not afraid of love! Love I embrace unguarded—and I love Allison! I want her, Gil!

GIL *(Also rises.)* Yeah, well, so do I!

LENNY *(Face to face.)* Yeah? Well . . . well . . . well, step outside.

GIL Why? *(Shakes his head.)* You wanna fight?

LENNY No. *(Beat.)* I just want you to step outside. *(ALLISON enters.)* Al!

GIL *(Whirls around to face her.)* Al!

ALLISON *(Coming over.)* Hi, hi—Lenny, what a surprise!

GIL You're late.

ALLISON Oh, I'm sorry. The rain—

LENNY That's all right.

GIL I was worried—

LENNY So was I.

GIL —cuz Lenny has to go.

ALLISON Oh no, do you really? *(GIL and LENNY speak at the same time.)*

LENNY No, not really.

GIL Yeah, he does. *(Beat.)* You look great, Al.

ALLISON *(Almost shyly, loves this.)* Do I? You don't think I gained a little weight?

GIL No, baby—*(Meaningful beat.)*—and it wouldn't matter if you did.

(They gaze into each other's eyes.)

LENNY *(Witnessing their passion.)* Actually, I really should be getting back . . . you know, to my empty apartment.

GIL Here—*(Reaches.)*—let me hang up your coat. *(He helps her out of it, hugs her tenderly.)*

ALLISON *(Lovingly)* Thanks, Gilly. *(Turns back to* LENNY.*)* Well, Len, listen, we have to get together *soon.*

LENNY Yeah . . . *(Sadly)* . . . soon.

GIL Soon. *(Loud and clear)* We'll see ya, Lenny.

LENNY Yeah. See ya. *(He extends hand to* GIL. GIL *hesitates a second, then shakes, smiles.* LENNY *turns mournfully to* ALLISON.*)* Goodbye, Al. *(He turns, walks toward the door as* GIL *leaves to hang up her coat. When* GIL *is out of sight,* LENNY *turns back, gives* AL *the okay sign. She smiles huge, signs it back to him. He smiles, turns around, seems very sad, leaves. Blackout.)*

The "I" Word: Interns

'99

> MICHAEL LOUIS WELLS

ORIGINAL PRODUCTION

DIRECTOR Jamie Richards
ASSISTANT DIRECTOR Heather Ondersma
SET DESIGNER Kenichi Toki
COSTUME DESIGNER Amela Baksic
SOUND Beatrice Terry
PROPS Erika Malone
PRODUCTION STAGE MANAGER Gretchen A. Knowlton
STAGE MANAGER Rachel Putnam

The cast was as follows:
KYLIE Sarah Rose
GEORGE Ian Reed Kesler
BARROW Kerry Butler
JAN Katherine Leask

CHARACTERS

KYLIE a scrappy young woman in her early twenties

GEORGE a bright, earnest young man about the same age

BARROW a young woman about the same age working her last
   day

JAN their boss, an intense woman in her forties

PLACE

A small room in the Old Executive Office Building

TIME

Late on the evening of September 16, 1998

NOTE

On Wednesday, September 16, 1998, President Clinton received
President Vaclav Havel of the Czech Republic at the White House.
The two addressed the crowd and took questions from the press at
the State Department. That evening a State Dinner was held at the
White House. Lou Reed performed.

*In black the sounds of Fleetwood Mac's "Don't Stop." At rise we discover a
small room in the Old Executive Office Building on a floor shared by staff
and interns of the White House Communications Office and the Office of the
Press Secretary. The furniture and surroundings have the feel of eclecticism,
suggesting both the grandeur of the building and the crammed workspace
that's been carved out of it by necessity. A beautiful wooden desk down left
with a computer and printer atop it is littered with papers. Another*

smaller desk, maybe purchased from Staples, sits up right near a window abutted by inexpensive metal filing cabinets. An exquisite wooden bookcase up center lists forward under the weight of reference books that fill its shelves. Gray industrial carpeting covers the floor. Three castered office chairs sit behind and beside the two desks. An antique map of Washington and a photograph of President Clinton adorn the walls. A door with a frosted windowpane and a transom leads to a hallway. Moonlight streams through the window blinds, dimly illuminating the room.

GEORGE *and* KYLIE, *two young interns for the Office of the Press Secretary, enter. Both wear pink passes with a bold* I *embossed in the center around their necks.* GEORGE *hits a light switch and fluorescent lights flicker to life.* KYLIE's *carrying a copy of today's* Washington Post. *They're in mid-conversation.*

KYLIE I feel like I'm lookin' at a different person now.

GEORGE Kylie . . .

KYLIE I wonder do I even know ya?!

GEORGE It was a long time ago . . .

KYLIE And what else . . . ?

GEORGE It was before I even knew ya!

KYLIE What else is back there I don't know about 'cause you're scared to tell me?!

GEORGE Of course I'm scared to tell you! The whole thing's mortifying, but I knew I hadta.

KYLIE Fuckin' . . .

GEORGE I knew I should.

KYLIE . . . Beige Girl.

GEORGE Even though there's never been any question you're no fan of hers. *(Beat.)* Where's the file on the IMF?

KYLIE Key in G-7.

GEORGE Right. *(He punches it up on his desktop.)* We don't even know if anything happened.

KYLIE I'm supposed to believe that, George? You wake up in her *bed*?!

GEORGE *Alone*, okay?

KYLIE She's makin' coffee.

GEORGE Right. I pull on . . .

KYLIE Such bullshit.

GEORGE . . . clothes that smell like cigarettes soaked in Budweiser, my face burning, and stagger off into the . . . Hit print, willya?

(KYLIE prints the file. GEORGE riffles through papers at the other desk.)

KYLIE Ya never asked her about it?

GEORGE I don't wanna know.

KYLIE You're not the only one, but . . .

GEORGE Where's the . . . ?!

KYLIE . . . too late.

GEORGE Fuck. Oh, here it is.

KYLIE What could you possibly see in her?

GEORGE Just stop it!

KYLIE What?

GEORGE I can't do this right now. But if you wanna have it out later, I got a coupla . . .

KYLIE Huh?

GEORGE Why, after three months, d'we still gotta keep our whole relationship top secret still? Scared to death anyone here'll find out. Maybe that's somethin' worth lookin' at.

KYLIE It's different for women!

GEORGE I need . . .

KYLIE I don't want it lookin' like I'm only here to find some *guy* or something.

GEORGE Thanks a lot.

KYLIE What?

GEORGE So I'm just *some guy*. That's really swell.

KYLIE That's not . . .

GEORGE I need *Federalist*.

KYLIE Huh?

GEORGE That book you're sittin' on.

(KYLIE *hands over the book.* GEORGE *starts typing.*)

KYLIE I'm not playin' games with you, George, but I think I need some time to figure this all out.

GEORGE I can't do this now!

KYLIE Maybe we shouldn't see each other for a . . . George!

GEORGE What?

KYLIE What is this flurry of activity? Whatever you're doin', can't it wait till tomorrow?

GEORGE No! That's what I've been tryin' to tell ya! Why d'ya think I made the mad dash back over here?

KYLIE What's up?

GEORGE Jan pulled me aside at the reception. McCurry needs notes for tomorrow's briefing. Somebody in Frank's office tipped us the House is gonna release the videotape. Maybe by morning.

KYLIE What?! I thought we had till Monday.

GEORGE We don't know now. And we're not gonna get a look at it first. Mike's gotta go out there with something anticipating whatever it turns out to be. And if that's not enough . . .

KYLIE Yeah?

GEORGE I didn't have Havel's remarks from the thing today at State. Anything he said in Czech . . .

KYLIE The translation?

GEORGE I waited til six. Nothin', ya know? She only now, apparently . . . (*He is holding up the papers.*)

KYLIE Who?

GEORGE And there's this huge hole in the summary I hadta write around. Jan's gotta give that to McCurry for revisions and she's right behind us. She needs all this like *now*!

KYLIE Yeah, she'll have your ass. Ya better kick it.

GEORGE Like I don't know? Gimme a hand, willya?

KYLIE What?

GEORGE Proof my rough.

KYLIE Oh, stimulating.

GEORGE Please? *(KYLIE takes some pages from GEORGE.)* Christ, it's like bein' in a vise!

KYLIE What?

GEORGE He addresses the nation for four minutes. The press is breathin' down our neck, and he flees to Martha's Vineyard for two weeks. Today's his first bit on the record in months. I fuck this up and *I'm* toast! *(GEORGE is banging away at his keyboard. KYLIE's rooting around in her bag.)* Whaddya doin'?

KYLIE Crackin' a window.

GEORGE You're not gonna *smoke* in here, are ya? If Jan catches ya . . .

KYLIE Everyone's gone. I'm not sneakin' out for the furtive puff.

GEORGE It's policy. Even the President hadta step out onto the Truman balcony for a "victory cigar."

KYLIE Somehow I don't imagine you're gonna be seein' him anywhere in the vicinity of a Dutch Masters for a while.

GEORGE Ya can't wait ten minutes?

KYLIE No. And I don't feature paddin' outta here alone at this hour.

GEORGE Ya shouldn't. There's a lotta crazy people out there.

KYLIE Yeah, and any number of rogue media types . . .

GEORGE Huh?

KYLIE . . . tryin' to squeeze one more word outta . . .

GEORGE An unnamed White House source?

KYLIE Yeah. They're a lot scarier than some mugger or whatev.

GEORGE Shit!

KYLIE What?

GEORGE This is all . . . Fuck! I know this isn't right.

KYLIE What's the matter?

GEORGE Did *he* say this or . . . It's not attributed.

KYLIE I was at State today. Show me.

GEORGE This bit. Is it backward or . . . ?

KYLIE Yeah. It's transposed. He said all this in English. They asked him in Czech and then . . . Man, this *is* fucked up. Later. *(Beat.)* Okay, *here*. Right? He waved off the interpreter—Havel—and answered this in English. He made that joke.

GEORGE About Sosa and McGuire.

KYLIE Here, yeah.

GEORGE Right.

KYLIE How could anyone fuck this up so bad? All they had to do was type in the . . .

GEORGE Yeah.

KYLIE And then run it over here. Who did this, anyway?

GEORGE Uh . . .

KYLIE *(Beat.)* Don't even tell me I'm helpin' you fix *her* screw-up! Charming. Beige Girl.

GEORGE Why d'ya . . . ?

KYLIE What color would you call her hair?

GEORGE Barrow? I dunno. Blondish?

KYLIE It's beige. Everything about her has this sorta pukey off-white aura. *(Beat.)* Wait a minute.

GEORGE What?

KYLIE You mean she's still *working* today?

GEORGE We had to bite the bullet.

KYLIE After this morning's . . . ?!

GEORGE We hadta let her finish her last day here as scheduled.

KYLIE She's a traitor!

GEORGE Erskine told Jan if we cut her loose even an hour before the end of the day it's all we hear about in the press for a week.

KYLIE This whole thing's bullshit!

GEORGE What can we do?

KYLIE If Miss Thing was so bugged and "wrestling with her conscience" after the President's speech, why didn't she quit that *day*?

GEORGE Why didn't everybody?

KYLIE What?

GEORGE I know why *I* didn't.

KYLIE Me too. That's why we're still here.

GEORGE As unpaid free-floating troubleshooters.

KYLIE That's the gig.

GEORGE Right.

KYLIE If ya don't believe ya . . .

GEORGE Get out that day.

KYLIE But Beige Girl. Whaddya think she's been doin' for three weeks?

GEORGE I dunno.

KYLIE Shoppin' her sad story . . .

GEORGE Ya think?

KYLIE What else, till she lands the *Post*! *(Holding up the paper.)* Mary McGrory fashions it into some searing indictment.

KYLIE AND GEORGE "Gen-Xers Betrayed."

KYLIE Christ! Yeah, and another fifteen-minute media star is born! She symbolizes everything that disgusts me!

GEORGE Kylie . . .

KYLIE The capital's crawlin' with opportunistic fuck-os like her! Playin' everyone around 'em just to get near celebrity or power. And then she turns out to be some *girlfriend* of yours!

GEORGE She wasn't ever . . .

KYLIE And it's still goin' on!

GEORGE What?!

KYLIE Battin' your eyelashes at her . . .

GEORGE C'mon!

KYLIE This smoldering ongoing vibe between ya I was too thick to put together till now. Don't tell me it's not there.

GEORGE None of this . . .

KYLIE So I'm crazy?

GEORGE . . . has anything . . .

KYLIE I'm a liar?

GEORGE . . . Kylie, to do with reality! One time, months before I met ya, I went out with her once, drank to unconsciousness, and can't . . .

KYLIE What?

GEORGE . . . remember a thing. The entire isolated incident's a blur.

KYLIE Whaddya mean once?

GEORGE Once. As in the one and only time . . .

KYLIE You said you went to the movies with her.

GEORGE What?

KYLIE You saw *Titanic.* Ya told me last night.

GEORGE Oh, right.

KYLIE What?!

GEORGE I forgot. I mean, it wasn't . . .

KYLIE George.

GEORGE . . . memorable. What?

KYLIE The sordid details aren't the point. It's the creepy way they keep changin' now ya tell me that makes me not trust you!

(There's a knock on the door.)

GEORGE Fuck! I'm not finished! *(He types furiously.* KYLIE *grabs her smokes.)* Yeah?

*(*BARROW *enters. She's a young woman about the same age as* GEORGE *and* KYLIE. *She's carrying a book.)*

BARROW Hey, George.

KYLIE Swell.

BARROW Oh, Kylie. You still here?

KYLIE Ditto.

BARROW Huh?

KYLIE Forget it.

BARROW Okay. So, George . . . ya wanna maybe go out for a drink or something? It's my last day and all.

GEORGE I can't, Barrow.

BARROW What?

GEORGE Really. We're under the gun and I gotta finish this.

BARROW *Now?*

GEORGE Yeah. Jan's gonna be here any minute. We thought you were her.

*(*BARROW *starts laughing uproariously.* GEORGE *and* KYLIE *eye each other.)*

BARROW Man, *that's* funny!

GEORGE Yeah, I guess. Anyway, it's not a good time.

BARROW Drag!

GEORGE Sorry.

BARROW Well, call me sometime, will ya? I wanna stay in touch.

KYLIE Uh-huh.

BARROW Great show, right?

KYLIE *You* were there?

BARROW Duh.

KYLIE Pardon?

BARROW Lou *Reed*? Think I'd miss that? No way.

KYLIE Who let you in?

BARROW Ya mean like where was I sitting?

KYLIE I mean who . . .

BARROW Great seats. This girl I just met from *Jane* magazine
brought me. She's coverin' it for . . .

KYLIE Uh-huh.

BARROW It was a little weird. But they're real nice.

KYLIE Who?

BARROW Ya know . . . the press.

KYLIE I'll bet.

BARROW I heard like Richard Butler was there.

GEORGE Yeah. Behind Havel, with the Joint Chiefs.

BARROW Wow. He's that guy from Love Spit Love, right?

KYLIE What?

BARROW And the Psychedelic Furs before that.

GEORGE No, that's the . . . uh . . . *other* one. This Richard Butler . . .

BARROW Yeah?

GEORGE . . . the one who was here tonight—he's the head of
UNSCOM.

BARROW What?

GEORGE He's the chief weapons inspector for the whole Iraqi . . .

KYLIE *(Incredulously)* God!

BARROW Oh. *(Beat.)* So they have like the same name?

GEORGE Yeah.

BARROW Small world.

KYLIE *(Hands* GEORGE *the papers.)* Your rough looks all right.

GEORGE Excellent. Thanks, Kylie.

KYLIE What else ya need?

GEORGE Nothin'. I just gotta gut this thing out now.

KYLIE Right.

BARROW Oh, I brought ya back that book ya lent me.

KYLIE What?

BARROW *No Ordinary Time.*

GEORGE Doris Kearns Goodwin.

BARROW Yeah. 'S great. Thanks. Did you know like President Roosevelt was in a wheelchair and stuff?

KYLIE No!

BARROW Seriously. He hadta overcome a lotta adversity. Anyway, here . . .

GEORGE Just put it on my . . .

BARROW There's a card inside.

KYLIE What?

BARROW Just to thank you for bein' nice to me and everything. You made it a lot easier to work around here, bein' my friend. This place can get pretty scary sometimes.

KYLIE I'm a little frightened right now.

(GEORGE *looks at the card. One side has writing. The other is a photograph of George Stephanopoulos.*)

GEORGE Uh . . . thanks.

BARROW You remind me of him kinda, ya know?

GEORGE George Stephanopoulos?

BARROW Especially when ya have your glasses on.

GEORGE I do?

BARROW Yeah. In a big way.

KYLIE Huh.

(GEORGE *and* KYLIE *exchange a glance.* GEORGE *removes his glasses.*)

BARROW It's not much, but I wanted to give ya somethin'.

KYLIE *Quid pro quo.*

BARROW Huh?

KYLIE Tits for tat.

GEORGE Kylie!

KYLIE You're a piece of work, ya know that?

BARROW What?

KYLIE You sell these lies of yours to the press . . .

BARROW Lies?!

KYLIE And then you have the balls to show up at the White House?!

BARROW It's the People's house.

KYLIE *Fuck* you.

GEORGE Kylie . . .

KYLIE I mean, who's responsible for lettin' you in. Where's the Secret Service when ya need 'em? Don't we have like sharpshooters for that?

BARROW This is exactly it! It's a war to you! Anyone who doesn't agree with ya's gotta watch their back!

KYLIE Oh, we demonize the opposition?

BARROW That's right.

KYLIE *We* didn't start that.

BARROW I saw you at the State Department today.

KYLIE How'dya get in there? Come along with George Will?

BARROW And if ya didn't have these *blinders* on you could see it!

KYLIE Just shut the fuck up.

BARROW Ya got these two men standin' there. The contrast is embarrassing.

KYLIE Spoken like a true embarrassment.

BARROW Havel can make some kinda moral argument 'cause he earned it. Speakin' out for his people when it was real danger. Even when they jailed him, leadin' a . . .

KYLIE Velvet Revolution.

BARROW Yeah! *(Beat.)* What?

GEORGE The movement in Czechoslovakia.

KYLIE They named it after the Velvet Underground.

GEORGE That's why Havel wanted Lou Reed here.

BARROW See? That's leadership.

KYLIE Huh?

BARROW Ya can't do that if you're only ever worried how you're doin' in some poll or something.

KYLIE He stands for something.

BARROW Yeah!

KYLIE And the fact that he *is* standing there . . .

BARROW Huh?

KYLIE . . . with the President. Does that provoke any thought in your little head? D'ya know why Havel is here? Did you listen to him at all?

BARROW Yes.

KYLIE And?

BARROW What?

KYLIE I'll give ya a clue. It's in that transcript ya fucked up.

BARROW I had to . . .

(KYLIE *grabs a paper off* GEORGE'*s desk.*)

GEORGE Hey, I need that!

KYLIE *(Reading)* "In modern times, Europe was the main exporter of world wars. Now it has a different chance: To build a new world. A peaceful world. I'm extremely grateful to the President. For his *leadership* made these chances open." Ring any bells?

BARROW Well, what else is he gonna say?

KYLIE How's that?

BARROW He doesn't wanna be rude, ya know? Besides, he's here for somethin'. Like ya said.

KYLIE So one minute Havel's your hero and the next . . .

BARROW No.

KYLIE . . . he's a beggar. Depending on what best advances your . . .

GEORGE Kylie . . .

KYLIE What? Oh, sorry. Here. *(She hands the page back to* GEORGE.*)*
It's easy to be outraged if ya don't have any ideas, Barrow.

BARROW You are so *mean*.

KYLIE How can I take you seriously now when your whole tenure
here reads like: Nowhere to be seen if we were late with a policy
paper but always at the front of a rope line if an actor dropped
by the Rose Garden?

BARROW He lied.

KYLIE What?

BARROW My President lied to me.

KYLIE Howd'ya know he lied? Have you read his testimony?

BARROW Legally accurate? You hang the whole thing on that?

KYLIE He's not your daddy or something, Barrow. For godsake!

BARROW No, not for godsake. For his own sorry sake, Kylie!

KYLIE Oh, touché.

BARROW And you with this bunker mentality still defending him!
D'ya think he'd do the same for you? How about Lani Guinier?
Whaddabout Joycelyn Elders?

KYLIE So ya've had a go at international affairs, now ya wanna . . .

BARROW Huh?

KYLIE . . . turn to the domestic? Okay, bonehead . . .

BARROW They were his *friends*, Kylie.

KYLIE And you've just now heard of them, apparently.

BARROW So . . .?

KYLIE Activists agitate. It's their job. And it's the job of *governing* . . .

BARROW Oh, so . . .

KYLIE . . . to build consensus. Getting . . .

BARROW . . . regardless of principle . . .

KYLIE . . . as close to the ideal . . .

BARROW I can't believe . . .

KYLIE . . . as you can achieve.

BARROW . . . I'm hearin', actually hearin' you . . .

KYLIE If you don't understand that, you don't belong in government, Barrow. You . . .

BARROW George?

KYLIE . . . belong—Don't look to him now . . .

GEORGE That's good.

KYLIE You belong—shut up—on Ricki Lake, screamin' at some hapless strawman guest with the rest of the moronic cross section of yaboes they've selected for today's audience.

BARROW That's so telling.

KYLIE It's a swell bloodletting, and you can feel all self-righteous good about yourself after, but you accomplish zilch. And nothing gets learned.

BARROW You really don't like people, do you?

KYLIE What people?

BARROW They're not even real to you. They're just this inconvenient mob of idiots that you're tryin' to get to do what you want, 'cause you think you know better than them what's good for us all!

KYLIE Why were you ever here?

BARROW Like I don't have a right or . . . ?

KYLIE No, no! Why *here*? Is there any difference for you . . . ?

BARROW What?

KYLIE . . . between running papers here or on the Hill for, like . . .

GEORGE Dick Armey.

KYLIE God, could he *have* a better name?!

GEORGE I know.

KYLIE They should just scrap the whole GOP tag and all of 'em run under *that*!

BARROW This is exactly . . .

KYLIE Do you have even one core belief that leads you to this place?

BARROW Do you?

KYLIE What?

BARROW Maybe I don't have the answers all worked out yet personally for myself . . .

KYLIE "Personally for myself"?

BARROW But what's so sophisticated about just adopting some political like guidelines because somebody told you that's what ya gotta think if . . . that's what "smart" people are supposed to believe? It must be a sad life.

KYLIE What?!

BARROW It must be, if you only live it according to this political agenda that takes up everything you are. How can you be a person? A woman . . .

KYLIE Shut up!

BARROW . . . if all the normal things ya need, like love and sex and babies, are nothing to you but something in somebody else's bill you're pushin'. Some wedge issue. It's pretty scary.

KYLIE You don't know the first . . .

BARROW You're scary. Every man around here is terrified of you. You're like shrill. I don't think guys like that.

GEORGE Barrow, knock it off!

BARROW It's not 'cause I'm leavin' it bugs you.

KYLIE There's the door.

BARROW Somehow I'm not even sure you know why I threaten you.

KYLIE *Threaten?*

BARROW 'S my relationship with George, I guess. But . . .

GEORGE What?

KYLIE Your *relationship*?

BARROW Right?

KYLIE What relationship?

BARROW I dunno. What's he told ya?

GEORGE Barrow!

BARROW It's none of my business.

GEORGE Barrow, c'mon!

BARROW It's not. But you're right, Kylie. I don't belong here. Not if that's what it costs.

KYLIE Let's try this again.

BARROW Huh?

KYLIE Why were you *ever* here?

BARROW Because . . .

KYLIE For *this* President if . . .

BARROW Because he said things . . .

KYLIE What?

BARROW . . . I didn't even know I believed, and so beautiful, made me wanna follow him. In '92. He was *my* guy then, too.

KYLIE In '92?

BARROW He was.

KYLIE When you were fifteen.

BARROW So? I saw *The War Room* . . .

KYLIE Oh, for fuck's . . .

BARROW . . . about a hundred . . .

KYLIE . . . sake!

BARROW . . . times. I get choked up . . .

KYLIE God!

BARROW . . . even *thinkin'* about it! Those guys were my heroes. I wanted to *be* them.

GEORGE Yeah.

BARROW Right? Remember at the end? It's the last day. Everyone's crammed into that room in Little Rock. And Stephanopoulos is tellin' 'em for the first time in forever they're gonna win tomorrow. Carville's just *shaking*. He's been waiting for this his whole life. Like all the old people.

KYLIE Old people?

BARROW Yeah. He's like *forty* or somethin'. He's so shook up he can barely get the words out tellin' the new ones, the kids there like us, how special they are. That he'll never forget "all y'all" because they made it different this time. They gave their . . .

GEORGE Labor.

BARROW Yeah. And their . . .

GEORGE Love.

BARROW Right. For something bigger, and in a way that's sacred.

KYLIE He's talkin' about . . .

BARROW That he's *proud* of them. 'Cause there's no greater gift than that. He starts cryin'. Me too. That's right where I always lose it.

KYLIE Do you even know . . . ?

BARROW 'Cause that woke somethin' up in my heart that, okay, maybe I don't understand, but . . .

KYLIE That's exactly . . .

BARROW . . . that I believed. It made me come here. Like some holy war for . . .

KYLIE *Ideas.*

BARROW Maybe, but . . .

KYLIE That's what all the tears are about. It's the *ideas* that are . . .

BARROW Sacred?

KYLIE Yes! Yes! And that's . . .

BARROW So where are they?

KYLIE What?

BARROW Does anybody around here even know? 'Cause I don't. A war is *all* it is now. And there's nothin' . . .

KYLIE That's not . . .

BARROW . . . holy in it. All my friends, my family, I thought would be proud of me, are just embarrassed. Ashamed. You're not the only one, Kylie. They think I'm an idiot, too. Because I thought this was so important. I believed him.

KYLIE Well . . .

BARROW I believed *in* him.

(BARROW *covers her face with her hands.* GEORGE *has stopped working and is staring off into space, thinking.* KYLIE's *slumped into a chair. No one speaks for a long moment.*)

BARROW *(Beat.)* I'm sorry. I didn't mean to . . .

GEORGE What?

BARROW I *like* you guys. *(Beat.)* Kylie?

KYLIE Leave me alone. George, are you done?

GEORGE What? Oh yeah. I just gotta . . .

KYLIE Right, then.

GEORGE . . . print.

BARROW Why don't you guys come out? Ya know? Kylie . . . ? *(Beat.)* George, ya wanna?

GEORGE No, you go ahead.

BARROW Will ya call me?

GEORGE I don't think that's such a great idea.

BARROW Why not?

GEORGE I'm seein' Kylie now and . . .

KYLIE Don't drag me into this.

BARROW I just mean like friends, is all.

GEORGE I don't think it's a great idea.

BARROW Man! *(Beat.)* Nothing happened, ya know.

KYLIE Huh?

BARROW I just said that before 'cause I was mad at you.

KYLIE You *what?!*

BARROW Everyone knows you guys are sleeping together. It's not like a big secret.

KYLIE *(Beat.)* C'mere.

BARROW What?

KYLIE I'm gonna pull every beige hair outta your tiny fuckin' . . .

BARROW George . . . !

(KYLIE lunges at BARROW. The door bangs open. JAN, an enigmatic woman in her late forties, enters. GEORGE jumps up and hits the printer. KYLIE and BARROW freeze.)

JAN Ms. Reynolds . . .

BARROW Hi, Jan.

JAN I don't believe you work here anymore.

BARROW Ummm. I don't. I was just . . .

JAN Yeah?

BARROW I was just saying goodbye.

JAN Well, it's late. And you're in a restricted area with that press pass.

BARROW Oh.

JAN We've got a long day ahead and I'd like to talk to my staff, if you don't mind.

KYLIE *(Sotto voce)* Staff?

BARROW I'm just leaving.

JAN Uh-huh.

BARROW Bye, George.

(GEORGE looks over quickly.)

GEORGE See ya.

BARROW Think about it, okay?

JAN Ms. Reynolds.

BARROW Right. I'm off.

(BARROW goes to the door. She stops, looking back soulfully at GEORGE. He doesn't see her. JAN does, and gives her a withering stare. BARROW wilts a bit and scurries off. JAN closes the door.)

JAN What a twit.

GEORGE Huh?

JAN George! Pages!

GEORGE Comin' up.

(GEORGE begins gathering up the release as the printer spits it out. JAN looks around. She makes a face.)

JAN Has somebody been smoking in here?

GEORGE Uh . . .

JAN Kylie?

KYLIE Huh?

JAN What ya packin'?

KYLIE Pardon?

JAN Gimme a smoke, willya?

GEORGE Huh?

JAN It's all right. We'll crack a window.

GEORGE Right.

(KYLIE hands JAN the pack of cigarettes.)

KYLIE Here.

JAN Dunhills.

KYLIE Yeah.

JAN Very posh.

(GEORGE hands JAN another page as KYLIE lights her up. JAN sits in the windowsill smoking and looking over the brief.)

JAN *(Not looking up.)* So, we're here late again.

GEORGE Yeah, I'm sorry this wasn't . . .

JAN No, no. I got hung up, too.

GEORGE Reporters?

JAN Ya gotta say the same thing five different ways to these bone-heads before their little brains finally clear. I didn't think I was ever gonna get outta there.

GEORGE Who was it?

JAN Some troll from TNR.

*(*GEORGE *continues to hand* JAN *pages. She speaks while reading, seldom looking up.)*

GEORGE Here.

JAN Thanks. I guess because we actually speak in complete sentences instead of the garbled syntax of the last bunch here, they suspect we must be up to no good. Quayle's announcing.

GEORGE For 2000?

JAN *(Nods.)* Bring him on! We won't hafta go through all this. *(She's indicating the transcript.)* I'll just hold up a potato.

GEORGE Right.

JAN They can't help themselves, I guess.

GEORGE Who?

JAN The Fourth Estate. They're so stung by the liberal-media charge, they'll bend over backward now to hand the mike to the other side of the aisle. Of course the GOP's horrible secret is they're best in opposition. They don't know what to do with their flimsy majority. They'd like to blame that on somebody, too, and we're right handy. Like if they distract us all long enough, maybe they'll come up with something and get into the swing of it. So, for us . . . Pages, George!

GEORGE Sorry.

JAN . . . in the time it takes to point all this out daily and still get back on message, we gotta speed at ten times the rhetorical threshold that used to pass muster. Ya know?

GEORGE Uh . . .

JAN We negotiate every roadblock, and then it comes out: "White House Spin Machine Floats Illusion of Business as Usual."

GEORGE Right.

JAN It's no damn illusion. That's what it takes to get your work done around here now. We actually survive this absurdly inhospitable climate they make us, and still they're deaf to the irony. *(Beat. She looks up.)* Huh . . .

GEORGE What's wrong?

JAN I've been thinkin' all this for weeks—like drivin' in with the Beloved or pickin' up the kids—but it's the first time, I think, I've actually said it out loud. This whole mess is funny that way. *(Beat.)* What's up with you two hot shots?

GEORGE Huh?

JAN You're unusually subdued. Please don't tell me Ms. Miracle of Science has just bollixed you up here with some of her fabulous new insights.

GEORGE Well . . .

JAN This is no time for the faint of heart. If you're havin' any doubts I wanna hear 'em.

GEORGE Not exactly, but . . .

JAN Men are weak. I'm sure you'll agree with me, George.

GEORGE Uh . . .

JAN We all do stupid things. Not usually as infuriatingly irresponsible as . . .

GEORGE Well . . .

JAN When one of us fucks up it doesn't usually tend to cripple an entire year of policy initiative. But why we're here, I would presume, is bigger than any single one of us alone.

KYLIE Yeah?

JAN Don't be thick. If that were true, even with one perfect standard bearer you'd have eight years to complete the venture, and that's it. Case closed. It doesn't work that way.

GEORGE Yeah.

JAN Ya don't raise a *child* in eight years. Why would you think . . .

KYLIE Right.

JAN It's a lifetime of work. If you're up for it, I mean. Are ya?

GEORGE I think so.

JAN Well, *know* so, willya? I need ya upstairs.

GEORGE Huh?

JAN Both of you firebrands. I got two slots. You're on staff. I mean, if you're up for it.

GEORGE Starting when?

JAN October 1, officially. But I need some new blood over at State now. *(Beat.)* What, you're in shock?

GEORGE No, just . . .

JAN Think about it. Tell me tomorrow. Am I missing a page?

GEORGE Uh . . .

JAN No, it's outta order. Got it. So what's the deal with this music tonight?

GEORGE You didn't like it?

JAN 'S all right, I guess. He can't really *sing*, can he?

GEORGE Lou Reed?

JAN Yeah. Am I missing something?

GEORGE Maybe so.

JAN Am I?

GEORGE The "singing" . . . the *melody*, ya know—it's not really the point.

JAN No?

GEORGE He just . . . He *means* it. He sorta *is* the song.

JAN Yeah, yeah. Like Dylan, right?

GEORGE Sure. Sorta.

JAN I get ya. Every generation has theirs. I'm a child of the sixties. My taste runs more to the Beatles. Fleetwood Mac.

KYLIE *(Sotto voce)* God!

GEORGE The Beatles are good.

JAN This bit from *Federalist* is good, George.

GEORGE Thanks.

JAN And these Havel quotes. The one about America being a big body with many faces. Most of which he loves. Some he doesn't understand. And that he doesn't like to speak . . .

KYLIE ". . . about things I don't understand."

JAN Brilliant. If we could only administer that into the oath before the next Congress take their seats.

GEORGE Right.

JAN What's this bit about a "civic" society?

GEORGE That was Kylie's idea.

KYLIE Huh?

GEORGE It was. That thing you read before made me dig back into his remarks and . . .

JAN "Civic"? Doesn't he mean civil?

GEORGE It's a conflation.

JAN A . . . ?

GEORGE In Czech. I looked it up. We don't have one word that translates well, so he's using it in the archaic to mean "humane or tolerant" and "a governing body"—the state, ya know that's responsible for it—simultaneously. So, "One of my personal whole life ideals is the ideal . . ."

JAN "Of a civic society."

GEORGE Right.

JAN "I must tell you that the America I know of President Clinton is for my work for a civic society, a big inspiration." That's good.

KYLIE Yeah.

JAN They'll never believe we didn't *pay* him to say that, but it's good. All of it.

GEORGE Thanks.

JAN McCurry should just read it verbatim tomorrow. Maybe it'll get 'em off our neck.

KYLIE You're not worried about the . . . ?

JAN Video release?

KYLIE Yeah.

JAN We *all* are. Who knows what's on there? But it might break our way.

GEORGE Whaddya mean?

JAN This is what I wished he'd do all along. Get out from behind Legal and let everybody hear him. He's his own best advocate. Last month's disaster notwithstanding. *(Beat.)* How'd he look today, Kylie?

KYLIE At State? Whipped. Just *tired*, ya know? Until . . .

JAN Yeah?

KYLIE They're just throwin' these really loaded questions at him, trying to ignite some flash of the famous presidential temper. Like "Would you consider resigning if it got to be too much?" or "D'ya think you have the . . ."

JAN "Moral authority?"

KYLIE Yeah.

JAN *(Shaking her head, muttering.)* Donaldson . . .

KYLIE ". . . to lead?" But he wouldn't take the bait. He just got real calm, thoughtful, ya know, and said, "I believe that's something you have to demonstrate every day."

JAN Nice. *(Beat.)* What do you think that means? Kylie?

KYLIE Um . . . maybe . . . uh . . .

JAN Yeah?

KYLIE Maybe . . . Well, it's their job to make news, isn't it? But maybe we've taken the media's impulse to get a finger on the one *thing* . . . the . . . ya know . . .

JAN Disaster?

KYLIE Or triumph, yeah, that's supposed to explain it all, too much to heart. 'Cause, uh . . . uh . . .

JAN *(Beat.)* You're losin' it. George?

GEORGE No, she's got it. It's just *given that*, like Kylie's sayin', it's easy to forget that more important thing that . . .

KYLIE Gets you outta bed every morning.

JAN Right.

KYLIE Whether or not you're the kind of person anyone's trackin' for posterity, we all have that.

JAN Uh-huh. *And?*

KYLIE And . . . uh . . .

GEORGE *(Beat.)* You need to keep it out front for yourself?

JAN That's it. *(Beat.)* You can take a breath now, Kylie.

KYLIE *(Sotto voce)* Man!

JAN All right. Good work today. Both of you.

GEORGE Thanks.

JAN Just keep your head, you.

KYLIE Huh?

JAN I heard how you handled "Boy Wonder" from *The Standard*.

KYLIE Who told ya?

JAN Never mind. Just don't let 'em rattle you. The squeeze is on.

KYLIE Right. Sorry.

JAN No. Ya did good. Just . . .

KYLIE Remember to smile?

JAN If a grimace will do, yeah. I'm not sayin' it's easy, but . . .

KYLIE Right.

GEORGE Jan, can I ask you somethin'?

JAN Shoot.

GEORGE Was it different? Ya know, all this, in the sixties?

KYLIE Oh brother.

JAN Yeah. Of course. For one thing, I wouldn't've had a job like this.

GEORGE No?

JAN No way. That's somethin' you oughta remember, Kylie.

KYLIE Me?

JAN It was very hard for a woman to be taken seriously in this town. That didn't happen overnight, ya know. A lotta bodies went down over the barricades so the likes of you could have an equal right to mouth off. So you could . . .

KYLIE Yeah?

JAN . . . perfect your dissy style. *(Beat.)* Did I use that correctly?

KYLIE What?

JAN "Dissy." To dis. "You dissin' me?"

KYLIE Uh, yeah. Perfect usage.

JAN All right, let's get outta here, people. It's gonna be another long one tomorrow.

KYLIE Just for something different.

GEORGE Jan?

JAN Let's go.

GEORGE Did you really intern for R.F.K.?

JAN George . . .

GEORGE Sorry, I just . . .

JAN I'm not like the History Channel, ya know. Another time we'll get into this. Have a drink or something. Now it's late and . . .

GEORGE Right.

JAN *(Beat.)* One thing, though. And no one remembers this. People didn't like him.

GEORGE Bobby Kennedy?

JAN Some did, of course. I loved him. But there was no middle ground. You either worshipped the man or reviled him.

KYLIE Sounds familiar.

JAN It should. That "Third Way" text you're working on for the symposium with Prime Minister Blair? It's not a new idea. The senator was working along those lines thirty years ago.

GEORGE Third Way?

JAN Third *rail*. It's a good idea *and* political dynamite. People responded the same way then.

GEORGE In '68?

JAN He made some people feel very threatened. He had a lotta enemies. Even after California it was by no means clear had he . . . had he . . .

GEORGE *(Beat.)* Lived?

JAN It was by no means clear he'd become President. He might not've even been nominated.

GEORGE Like Woodstock.

KYLIE What?

GEORGE Half a million people showed up and another half a million *think* they did.

JAN Right. Time . . .

KYLIE Heals all loons.

JAN Let's hope so. Grab those butts, willya?

GEORGE Pardon?

JAN The cigarettes.

GEORGE Oh.

JAN Can't be too careful around here.

KYLIE Apparently.

JAN All right. See ya tomorrow.

GEORGE On four.

JAN Right. *(Beat.)* Both of you.

KYLIE Yes.

JAN Good. See ya. *(She exits.)*

KYLIE God!

GEORGE What?

KYLIE Every time she comes near me, my speech devolves to the submoronic!

GEORGE Whaddya talkin' about? You were great.

KYLIE Jan loves you, George. You'll probably be writing stump for Al next year if ya wanna.

GEORGE I dunno.

KYLIE You're good, George. Junior staff doesn't get to draft re-marks for policy unless they're headed onward and ever upward.

GEORGE That Blair thing? I'm just a wonk.

KYLIE C'mon.

GEORGE It's okay. I like it. You're the one, though.

KYLIE What?

GEORGE Why d'ya think she kicks your ass so hard? Jan?

KYLIE I wish I could believe that. I want this more than anything.

GEORGE Ya just got it.

KYLIE I know. I'm scared.

GEORGE Me too.

KYLIE I mean, this is for real now. I gotta be sure. *(Beat.)* Why couldn't I answer her?

GEORGE Who?

KYLIE Beige Girl. When she asked me . . .

GEORGE Where the ideas are?

KYLIE Why don't I know that?

GEORGE Ya do.

KYLIE I . . .

GEORGE We'll get there if we can. We'll *try*. If we don't make it, it's not gonna be because of *this*. Ya just gotta believe that he still has those things we both care about way deeper inside of him than any of this tawdry shit all up in our face now. Then you can sign on.

KYLIE If you're up for it.

GEORGE I'm not apologizing for him. I just feel I know that. Don't you?

KYLIE Yeah. It's just hard.

GEORGE I know.

KYLIE But I'm up for it.

GEORGE Same here.

KYLIE All right. *(Beat.)* Staff.

(They high-five.)

GEORGE *(Beat.)* So are we okay?

KYLIE Whaddya mean?

GEORGE I don't want to parse the statement.

KYLIE Well, if nothin' happened between you two, yeah. I *guess* we are. I dunno. It's just . . .

GEORGE Yeah?

KYLIE It's not even about that. I'm not supposed to meet you yet.

GEORGE What?

KYLIE You weren't supposed to come along till I was like thirty! Ya just totally fucked up all my plans.

GEORGE Sorry.

KYLIE Ya did!

GEORGE I know. But I want you.

KYLIE No kiddin'. You're like indefatigable. *(Beat.)* Ya wanna come over?

GEORGE To your place?

KYLIE Yeah. Maybe I can tire ya out.

(KYLIE's caught GEORGE up in an embrace. He moves in to kiss her. She breaks the clench.)

KYLIE Let's go.

GEORGE Okay.

KYLIE Ya know . . .

GEORGE Yeah?

KYLIE Ya do look a bit like Stephanopoulos.

GEORGE Shut up.

KYLIE In a Michael J. Fox kinda way.

(Blackout. Lou Reed's "Busload of Faith" comes up.)

Notes on Contributors

LESLIE AYVAZIAN is the author of *Nine Armenians,* which won the John Gassner Outer Critics award for best new play, the Susan Smith Blackburn award, and the Roger L. Stevens award; *Singer's Boy,* produced at A.C.T. in San Francisco; and several one-acts produced at E.S.T., including *Plan Day.* Her latest work, *High Dive,* a one-person performance piece, premiered in Fall 1999 at Trinity Repertory.

EDWARD ALLAN BAKER is the author of numerous plays produced Off and Off Off Broadway, including *Prairie Avenue.* He has also written for Showtime and HBO. His one-act play *Dolores* was published in *The Best Short Plays 1988–89.* He is a member of the Sarah Lawrence College theater faculty.

BILL BOZZONE has been a member of the Ensemble Studio Theatre since 1979. His last production at E.S.T., *Sonny DeRee's Life Flashes Before His Eyes* (Marathon '95), has since been produced across the United States, Canada, and, most recently, in England and Italy. He lives in Connecticut with his wife, novelist Tricia Bauer.

CHRISTINE FARRELL was the original creator and co-author of *Mama Drama,* which premiered at E.S.T. and has since been produced at regional theaters throughout the country. She teaches at Sarah Lawrence College, N.Y.U., and Playwrights Horizons Studio. She is often seen as the ballistics detective on *Law and Order.*

FRANK D. GILROY is a playwright, filmmaker, and novelist. In 1962, he received an Obie Award for *Who'll Save the Plowboy?* He received the Pulitzer Prize, the Tony Award, and the Drama Critics Circle Award in 1964 for *The Subject Was Roses. The Golf Ball* is his fourteenth one-act to be done at E.S.T.

SUSAN KIM's full-length plays include *Where It Came From, The Arrangement, Open Spaces,* and the stage adaptation of *The Joy Luck Club;* one-acts include *Pandora; Seventh Word, Four Syllables* (E.S.T. Marathon '93); *Rapid Eye Movement* (Marathon '91); *Death and the Maiden* (Marathon '90); and *Guts.* Kim has written extensively for television and received a Writer's Guild Award in 1997. She is a member of E.S.T. and the Dramatist's Guild.

ROMULUS LINNEY is the critically acclaimed author of three novels and numerous plays, including *The Sorrows of Frederick, Holy Ghosts,* and *Tennessee.* He has received both the Award in Literature and the Award of Merit Medal for Drama from the American Academy of Arts and Letters, and in 1992 he was awarded an Obie for sustained excellence in playwriting. His work is frequently produced at E.S.T.

CASSANDRA MEDLEY's plays include *Dearborn Heights, Waking Women, Ma Rose,* and *Ms. Mae,* one of several individual sketches that composed the Off Broadway musical *A . . . My Name Is Alice.* She was awarded a National Endowment for the Arts Grant in Playwriting in 1990 and won the New Professional Theatre Award in 1995. She teaches playwriting at Sarah Lawrence College and is a member of E.S.T.

STUART SPENCER's other works include *Water and Wine* (Marathon '96), for which *In the Western Garden* is the second act; *Blue Stars* (Marathon '92), which appeared in the *Best American Short Plays of 1993–94;* and *Resident Alien,* which has received numerous productions around the country and is in development as a motion picture. Spencer teaches playwriting at Sarah Lawrence College.

CHERIE VOGELSTEIN is the 1999 recipient of the then newly inaugurated James Hammerstein Fellowship for Best Emerging Playwright. A winner of the HBO Comedy Arts Festival Jury Prize in 1997, Ms. Vogelstein's comedies have been produced across the country. *All About Al* is her third play in the *Sex Over Coffee* collection, which includes *Cats and Dogs* (Marathon '95) and *Sisters* (Marathon '96). She is currently at work on *Bride-to-Be,* a full-length comedy about love, infidelity, and death.

MICHAEL LOUIS WELLS is the author as well of a full-length version of *The "I" Word: Interns.* Other short works include *Real Real Gone* (Marathon '97); *Friends?*, a finalist for the 1998 Actor's Theatre of Louisville National Ten-Minute Play Contest; and *A Brief History of Technology*, commissioned by the Albert P. Sloan Foundation for the 1999 First Light Festival. Presented regionally and in New York, his full-length works include *Seven Pages Unsigned*; *Taken by Faeries*; *Fourth Time Around*; and *District of Columbia*—currently in production at E.S.T.

Permissions